IBM Rational Business Developer
with EGL

Ben Margolis

MC PRESS

MC Press Online, LP
Lewisville, TX 75077

IBM Rational Business Developer with EGL

Ben Margolis

First Edition

First Printing—April 2008

MC Press offers excellent discounts on this book when orderd in quantity for bulk purchases or special sales, which may include custom covers and content particular to your business, training goals, marketing focus, and branding interest.

For information regarding permissions or special orders, please contact:
    MC Press
    Corporate offices
    125 N. Woodland Trail
    Lewisville, TX 75077 USA

For information regarding sales and/or customer service, please contact:
    MC Press
    P.O. Box 4300
    Big Sandy, TX 75755-4300 USA

ISBN: 978-158347-066-4

To Orly, who persevered.

Contents

Foreword

Hayden Lindsey, IBM Vice President

For years, IBM and other vendors have created sophisticated software to let organizations respond quickly to the marketplace. The unintended consequence? Complexity. The advances of the last decades provided many approaches, including various user-interface technologies, data-storage systems, transaction-control mechanisms, and communications software. Increasingly, business developers—the programmers who write enterprise applications—were asked to focus on narrow technical issues rather than on a business domain such as banking, insurance, or health care.

Business developers will always need to understand coding techniques such as looping and conditional processing, as well as issues of presentation and database access. But if we can shield developers from excessive technical detail, they'll be able to interact more effectively with executives, business analysts, and other personnel to provide solutions that reflect an organization's needs. The changing details of runtime technologies can be handled automatically and in a way that reflects a developer's general intent.

The nature of business software suggests a way forward. Applications are frequently based on one or more patterns, which can be the basis of generated logic. For example, most applications access data from a database or file system, present the data to the user, validate changes, and write the user's input to the original database or file location.

Software generators have been important since the 1950s. Early computer scientists had trouble coding in the 0s and 1s of machine language and created assemblers, which generated statements that were specific to a particular kind of machine. The same principle guided the development of compilers, which accepted logic written in a language such as COBOL or RPG and generated output for one or another platform. The intent in all cases was to let developers focus on higher-level issues—where to get data, how to manipulate it, where to store it—rather than on the most technical detail.

IBM® Rational® Business Developer (RBD) is a development environment that continues the trend. To address the complexity of modern software, RBD features a software generator and a new source-code language, EGL, as well as tools for handling development tasks quickly. With this solution, business developers don't need to track changes to complex systems such as Java™ Enterprise Edition (JEE) or Customer Information Control System (CICS®), but can focus on business logic.

EGL is based on customizable data types and logic units that a developer can learn easily. The elegance of the design is a tribute to Chief Architect Tim Wilson and a team of more than 30 engineers, testers, and usability experts who revamped the immediate predecessor language, VisualAge Generator.

EGL is well established—several thousand enterprises use a predecessor language for essential applications—yet the language is current, with extensive support for service development and access. A preview of Web 2.0 capabilities is now available as well, enabling a new level of developer creativity. And EGL supports the direct access of runtime technologies, Java objects, and JavaScript™ logic from the developer's code.

EGL is extensible. The language's data-access statements are designed for use with persistent storage of any kind so that new kinds of storage can be accommodated. Similarly, the logic units called *handlers* are designed to let developers interact with future user-interface technologies in much the same way as EGL handlers access current technologies.

IBM recognizes the difficulty an organization has in switching from one language to another. For almost three decades, we've provided upward compatibility for the languages that preceded EGL. We successfully protected our customers' investment in the code that was developed with those languages, and IBM intends to maintain that record. We also plan to give EGL developers and generation experts the ability to extend this language, further ensuring that EGL will support technologies yet unknown.

And there's more. IBM is working with an open-standards organization, the Object Management Group (OMG), to establish core aspects of EGL as a standard for use in Model Driven Development (MDD). Here's the potential result: After an analyst describes a business activity in Unified Modeling Language (UML), the analyst's work becomes an input to an MDD process that creates skeletal EGL source code. This use of EGL could bring further productivity gains.

IBM Rational Business Developer with EGL gives a clear introduction to an IBM product that represents the latest in generation technology. You may find that the book is like Rational Business Developer itself: a tool that simplifies.

Hayden Lindsey
Vice President and Distinguished Engineer
IBM Software Group
Rational Division, Enterprise Tools and Compilers

Acknowledgements

Many people helped to fashion this book, and the author's thanks go to all: to Jeri Petersen, who smilingly taught the details; to Tim Wilson, who offered a vision; and to Susan LaFera and Ralph Earle, who provided a detailed vision of their own, years ago.

Orly Margolis's illustrations and technical expertise were essential.

Let the gurus be honored: Dan Bruce, Bob Gallagher, David Murray, Alex Lui, Matt Heitz, Paul Hoffman, Chris Laffra, Brian Svihovec, Steve Dearth, Jon Shavor, Dev Banerjee, Mark Evans, Vince Petrillo, Amit Joglekar, Alice Connors, Jeff Douglas, Joe Vincens, Jonathan Sayles, Bob Cancilla, Guy Slade, Kevin Sloop, Justin Spadea, Paul Harmon, John Riendeau, Gregory Dietrich, Arlan Finestead, Eric Aker, Raj Daswani, Albert Ho, Lisa Lasher, and Henry Koch.

And thanks to my fellow gremlins: Tim McMackin, Susan Peich, Lewis Shiner, Brenda Roy, Debra Taylor, Gary Makely, Michael B. Schwartz, and Fred Borchers.

CHAPTER 1

Introduction

IBM Rational Business Developer (RBD) is a development environment that helps programmers write business applications quickly. An organization uses RBD to meet the following goals:

- Create applications that will be deployed on a single platform or across multiple platforms. The business logic can include programs, reusable function libraries, and modular units called *services*.

- Access business data from a variety of sources on a variety of platforms, even when programmers lack the detailed knowledge usually required for such access.

- Interact with a user by way of a Web browser, workstation window, or terminal emulator. All of these interfaces are available even to programmers who have little experience with the specialized systems that make possible the user-code interaction.

RBD supports EGL, a high-level language that lets developers create business software without requiring them to have a detailed knowledge of runtime technologies or to be familiar with object-oriented programming. Developers can focus on business issues, and your company can retain those people and their business savvy as technology changes.

EGL is the culmination of more than 25 years' experience in designing syntax for rapid application development. The language builds on its predecessors, offering a procedural syntax that supports recent innovations in database access, error handling, and data structure.

Like other Rational products, RBD is based on *Eclipse*, a publicly available, integrated development environment (IDE) that is described at *http://www.eclipse.org*. Developers familiar with Eclipse will be familiar with the most basic features of RBD. For example, RBD provides several *wizards*, each of which is a sequence of dialog boxes that elicit developer input. The input is then used to automate an aspect of the development process. Some wizards, akin to those in Eclipse, set up folders to contain the developer's source code. Other wizards go beyond the ones available in Eclipse, creating skeletal source code or Web pages.

The EGL developer writes and changes EGL source code in a text editor that provides typing assistance and other interactive help. The developer can use a source-code debugger to verify the code's runtime behavior and to test the effect of different data values. The debugging session switches seamlessly from technology to technology as the runtime situation changes. You might debug a program, for example, along with a service that is invoked by the program and is intended for use on a remote machine.

After the developer codes and debugs the EGL source, the next step is specific to EGL: with a keystroke, the developer submits the source as input to a process called *generation*. The primary output is Java or COBOL source code, which is the basis of an executable.

An additional generation option is based on emerging technology called *IBM Rational EGL Rich Web Support* (Rich UI), which (at this writing) is available only outside of Rational Business Developer. For Rich UI, you write EGL code and generate Web pages composed of Hypertext Markup Language (HTML) and embedded JavaScript.

The overall use of EGL is illustrated in Figure 1.1.

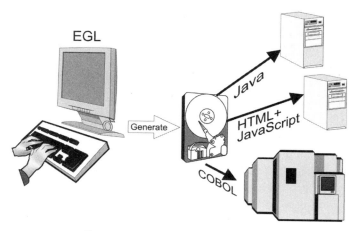

Figure 1.1: Generation and Deployment

An important aspect of code generation is that the output source has no lasting value. If you wish to make changes, you recode the EGL source and regenerate the output.

RBD can place the generated output on a deployment platform separate from the machine where development occurs. In the case of Java or COBOL output, the creation of an executable occurs on the deployment platform. EGL also produces supplementary files to help the deployment staff install the executable.

An EGL program written for one target platform can be easily configured for use on another. Developers can write code in response to current requirements, with most platform-specific details being handled by the generation process, not in the source. Developers also can create EGL software to run on one target platform and be assured that the code will retain its value if their company needs to migrate to a different target platform.

Another aspect of the overall development process is that RBD provides two ways to generate output. A developer working in the RBD workbench interacts with the capabilities described earlier, including editors, debuggers, and wizards. In contrast, a developer or administrator working with the EGL software development kit (SDK) uses a command-line interface that includes none of the interactive features characteristic of the RBD workbench.

An organization might use the SDK in an automated build process. Developers prepare an application for testing, for example, and then store the

EGL source files in a software-library system. A batch job periodically runs: first, to extract the files from the library system; second, to trigger generation; and third, to prepare and deploy the generated output. In response to errors found by the testers, the developers update and store the source code for another round of testing, which can occur only after the batch job runs again.

RBD runs on any of several Microsoft Windows platforms (Windows 2000®, Windows 2003®, Windows XP®, and Windows Vista®) or on Linux. The product includes WebSphere® Unit Test Environment, which is a component for *serving* (that is, transmitting) Web pages to browsers and for running applications under Java Enterprise Edition (JEE), which is described later. You can use the WebSphere environment to test Web and JEE applications as you develop them.

Support for Service-Oriented Architecture

Business processing increasingly relies on service-oriented architecture (SOA), which involves the deployment of accessible and more-or-less independent services, often on varied platforms. Rational Business Developer strongly supports the business use of SOA. EGL provides a language construct that is like a program but helps the developer to create a service; and the product provides ways to create and use a Web Services Description Language (WSDL) file, which tells how to access a service.

A service written in EGL can be deployed as a *Web service* or an *EGL service*. A Web service is widely accessible because it exchanges data that is in a text-based format called SOAP. In contrast, an EGL service uses a proprietary format for data exchange and so is directly accessible only to other EGL software. The main benefits of using an EGL service are first, it gives faster response than is possible with a Web service, and second, it reduces your company's need to maintain WSDL and related files.

EGL supports development and access of a third type of service, which conforms to Representational State Transfer (REST). REST is a style of service interaction and construction and typically uses a text-based format closely tied to traditional Web technology. At this writing, support for REST services is not in Rational Business Developer, but is part of the Rich UI offering.

Supported Technologies

A modern application relies on several technology domains:

- The runtime environment, which is software that determines what resources are available to the application and how the user invokes the application

- Persistent data storage, which includes the database and file systems from which an application reads data and to which the application writes data

- The user interface, which is an interactive mechanism for presenting data to the user and for receiving data from the user

- Network communication, which is a mechanism for transferring data between machines

- Report production, which is a mechanism for formatting business reports and presenting them to a screen or printer

- Integration with existing code

EGL is useful in relation to each domain, hiding many of the runtime details that would otherwise require your attention. You are rarely constrained by the conveniences that are offered, though. For example, when you write a user interface with Rich UI, you are likely to code only in EGL; but for advanced purposes, you can write custom JavaScript or access JavaScript libraries instead of relying on the default behavior of EGL.

The next sections describe the commercial technologies supported by EGL. The breadth of support has a long-term implication: the language and skills taught in this book are likely to remain useful even as your organization changes technologies.

Runtime Environment

EGL-generated code runs under any of the following environments.

- *Java Platform, Standard Edition (JSE)*. JSE is the simplest Java runtime. EGL-generated Java JSE code runs on the platforms AIX®,

HP UX, IBM i, Linux®, UNIX System Services (on System z™), and the supported Windows platforms.

- *Java Platform, Enterprise Edition (JEE)*. JEE is a Java runtime that provides special handling for database access, messaging, and Web applications. Developers can generate code that will run in one of the following three ways: first, as an *application client* (a Java program, but one that does not compete for all the resources needed to present data to a browser); second, in a *Web application* (logic that interacts with a browser); or third, as an *Enterprise JavaBean stateful session bean* (a modular unit of business logic). EGL-generated Java JEE code runs on the platforms AIX, HP UX, IBM i, Linux, Solaris®, UNIX System Services, and the supported Windows platforms.

  You can run JEE Web applications in Apache Tomcat, which you can download from *http://tomcat.apache.org*, and you can run any kind of Web or JEE application on WebSphere Application Server. EGL helps you to work with JEE security on either server.

- *IBM i*. On the midrange computer Power server (which uses the operating system IBM i), EGL-generated COBOL code includes interactive programs, batch programs, and services.

- *z/OS®*. On the mainframe computer System z (which uses the operating system z/OS), the EGL-generated COBOL code runs in any of the following environments:

  - *z/OS batch* is the z/OS batch-processing environment.

  - *Customer Information Control System (CICS)* is a *transaction manager*, which is a runtime for handling large numbers of business transactions such as customer orders. Developers can generate interactive programs, batch programs, and services, all in COBOL.

  - *Information Management System (IMS™)* is another transaction manager. Developers can generate COBOL programs that use any of the major IMS facilities on System z. Generated interactive programs can be IMS Message Processing programs (MPPs). Generated batch programs can be IMS Batch Message Processing programs (BMPs), DL/I

Batch programs, or MPPs. EGL also supports the IMS FastPath facility.

EGL offers a special benefit when you are writing interactive code for CICS or IMS. In this case, you structure your code as if the user were having a conversation with a program that is always in memory, even though the runtime code (in the usual case) is repeatedly brought into memory and taken out of memory during the program's interaction with the user. The complexity of the conversation is handled in the logic generated by EGL and not in your EGL source code, which is relatively simple to write and understand.

Persistent Data Storage

The EGL developer uses intuitive I/O statements (such as **add** and **get**) to access data from a relational database, a hierarchical database, a message queue, or a file:

- *Relational databases.* The standard language for accessing relational databases is Structured Query Language (SQL). For simple applications, the developer can rely on the SQL statements used by default in EGL I/O statements. For complex applications, an EGL developer familiar with SQL can go beyond the defaults. Moreover, EGL is structured so that an SQL developer can write sophisticated database-access code for other developers to use.

  EGL supports access of DB2® Universal Database (DB2 UDB) from COBOL code and supports access of the following databases by way of Java Database Connectivity (JDBC): DB2 UDB, Informix®, Microsoft SQL Server®, Oracle®, Cloudscape®, and Derby.

- *Hierarchical databases.* The standard language for accessing hierarchical databases is Data Language/I (DL/I). The developer can rely on default EGL I/O statements, can go beyond the defaults, and can write database-access code for other developers.

  EGL supports access of hierarchical databases on IMS, CICS, and z/OS batch.

- *WebSphere MQ message queues.* WebSphere MQ calls allow program-to-program communication that involves a set of queues managed by WebSphere MQ rather than by either program. The application that sends data is not dependent on the immediate availability of the application that receives the data, yet message delivery is assured.

When accessing a message queue, the EGL developer usually relies on default EGL I/O statements. Specialized expertise is not as necessary as in the case of database access.

EGL supports access of WebSphere MQ message queues on all platforms.

* *Files*. EGL supports access of *sequential files,* whose constituent records are accessed in record order. Access of those files is available for any target platform. EGL also supports access of two other types of files, for target platforms that allow the choice. Those other types are *indexed files*, whose records are each accessed by the value of a key in the record, and *relative files*, whose records are each accessed by an integer that represents the record's position in the file.

  For some platforms, you can associate a sequential, indexed, or relative file with any of several file technologies. You write your EGL code, then choose a file technology at generation time. The generated source code includes the I/O statements that are specific to the technology chosen.

  Here are the technologies:

  * *Virtual Storage Access Method (VSAM)*. EGL supports VSAM files, each of which is organized as a sequential, indexed, or relative file. EGL-generated code that runs on any of several platforms can access either local VSAM files or (in the case of IBM i) an equivalent type of file.

    The platforms for local access are AIX; IBM i; CICS; z/OS batch; and IMS (but only for EGL-generated BMPs on IMS). In addition, EGL-generated code that runs on a supported Windows platform can access VSAM files that reside on a remote System z.

  * *CICS-specific technologies*. EGL supports access of the following kinds of data stores on CICS: spool files, which primarily hold program output for subsequent printing;

temporary storage queues, which hold data for subsequent processing in the same or another program; and transient data queues, which submit data to another program.

- *IMS-specific technologies.* EGL supports using I/O statements to access *IMS message queues*, whether to submit data to another program or, in some cases, to retrieve data into a program.

    EGL also supports *Generalized Sequential Access Method (GSAM)* files, which are sequential files accessed by way of DL/I calls. Those calls allow processing to resume, after a failure, from the middle of a file rather than from the start.

    GSAM files are available to BMPs and on z/OS batch.

EGL supports access of two file types that are specific to IBM i: *physical files*, each of which contains data, and *logical files*, each of which provides a subset of the data in a physical file.

User Interface

With EGL, developers can create applications that interact with users in one of several ways, depending on the target system where the code runs. EGL supports a Web-based interface; a traditional character-based interface (for CICS COBOL, IMS COBOL, and Java applications); and a more interactive, largely character-based interface (for Java applications migrated from Informix 4GL).

Web-Based Interface

EGL supports Web-based interactions in three ways: first, by providing Rich UI, which is a new technology for writing applications that will be deployed on Web servers outside of JEE; second, by providing more complete support for JavaServer Faces (JSF), which is a well-established technology that runs on JEE; and third, by offering a migration path for the VisualAge Generator Web transaction, which also runs on JEE but is older and less flexible than the alternatives.

Each of the three mechanisms allows for elementary processing. The user can receive a Web page, type input into a form, and click a button to provide data for subsequent processing by application logic. Also, each mechanism allows a division of labor. A graphics designer who has minimal knowledge of software can create a Web page by dragging controls from a palette, dropping them on a drawing surface, and customizing them in a variety of ways.

Rich UI. In Rich UI, the application logic is EGL-generated JavaScript, which is called *client-side* because it runs in the browser, not on the remote machine that serves the Web page.

The important detail about client-side JavaScript is that it makes the Web page more responsive, providing greater flexibility so that the user's experience can go beyond receiving a page and submitting a form. Consider Figure 1.2, for example. After the user clicks a radio button, the code can respond by changing the content of a second control such as a textbox.

Figure 1.2: Example Use of JavaScript

The change occurs quickly because the logic runs locally and, in most cases, redraws only one area of the page.

An extension of client-side JavaScript is Asynchronous JavaScript and XML (AJAX), a technology that permits the runtime invocation of remote code and the subsequent update of a portion of a Web page, even as the user continues working elsewhere on the page. For example, after the user selects a purchase order from a list box, the JavaScript logic might request transmission of order-item details from the remote Web server and then place those details in a table displayed to the user. In this way, the application can access content from the server but can save time by selecting, at run time, which content is transmitted.

To work with Rich UI applications, you can download a non-JEE-compliant Web server such as the Apache HTTP server, which is available from *http://httpd.apache.org*. Alternatively, you can use a more powerful Web server such as Apache Tomcat or WebSphere Application Server.

JavaServer Faces (JSF). Many Web applications are not based primarily on client-side processing; instead, they are server-centric. Logic on a server guides the construction of a stream of HTML and transmits that stream to the browser. The user periodically submits data back to the server, which processes the input as appropriate and responds with another HTML stream.

An important technology for developing server-centric Web applications is *JavaServer Faces (JSF)*. JSF is a *framework*—a combination of development-time shortcuts and runtime logic. The framework provides convenience to the programmer, who can ignore commonplace issues that would otherwise drain time during development. After the JSF runtime detects a user error, for example, the JSF runtime redisplays the same Web page automatically, with the user's input still on display and with the first wrong input highlighted. In the absence of a framework like JSF, the developer would need to write customized logic to cause that behavior.

To guide the user-code interaction for a specific Web page, the developer writes an *EGL JSF handler*, which is composed of variables and functions. At run time, the handler specifies what kind of data is transmitted to and from the page, responds to the user's button clicks, and oversees input validation.

The EGL JSF handler resides in a JEE-compliant Web application server and runs under the control of the JSF runtime. Figure 1.3 illustrates the usual one-to-one relationship between a Web page and an EGL JSF handler.

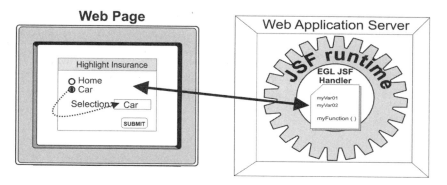

Figure 1.3: Web Page and the EGL JSF Handler

As suggested by the figure, JSF also supports client-side JavaScript and AJAX.

In general, server-side code can place user data in server memory, allowing a conversation with the user across multiple Web pages. The conversation can be affected by the code's access of databases that are available to the server.

A particular benefit of JSF is that decisions about the application flow—what page forwards to what other page—are not necessarily final at development time but can be deferred until the application is deployed. This ability to defer decisions adds to a company's flexibility because changes to the application flow may require only a change to a configuration file rather than new development.

Web transactions. As mentioned earlier, EGL also provides a third, less flexible way of serving business data to Web browsers. The developer in this case writes a program called a *Web transaction*, which is a pre-set flow of logic that transmits Web pages and receives data back. A JEE-compliant Web application server is required. The primary purpose of Web transactions is to migrate code from IBM VisualAge Generator.

Text UI

EGL-generated programs can process business logic and periodically display a *text form*—a set of character-based fields that are presented at a standalone terminal or in a workstation window. After displaying the form, the program waits for user input. A particular keystroke (ENTER or a specified function key) causes the program to receive the user's input and continue processing.

This interface technology is called *Text UI*. It provides support for interactive COBOL applications running on CICS, IBM i, or IMS. Text UI is also available for interactive Java applications; specifically, for JSE applications and JEE application clients. Use of this technology in Java is primarily to facilitate migration of the EGL code to and from the COBOL environments.

Console UI

EGL offers a user-interface mechanism called *Console UI*, primarily for code migrated from Informix 4GL. In this case, the users interact with buttons, drop-down lists, and the like, in a workstation window. Console UI is available for JSE applications and JEE application clients.

Network Communication

EGL lets your company avoid some of the effort needed to integrate logic that runs on different platforms. Specifically, your organization has less need to write *interface code*, which is software whose purpose at run time is illustrated in Figure 1.4.

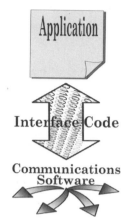

Figure 1.4: Interface Code

Interface code transfers application data to and from communications software, which in turn transmits the data from one platform to another. Your organization avoids the burden of writing interface code when EGL-generated Java logic calls a remote program deployed on IBM i, CICS, or IMS. Supported communications software for IBM i is IBM Toolbox for Java; for CICS, CICS Transaction Gateway; and for IMS, IMS Connector for Java.

Report Production

The EGL developer code can create output reports using either of several tools: Business Integration and Reporting Tools (BIRT), EGL text reporting, and print forms.

Business Intelligence and Reporting Tools (BIRT))

Business Intelligence and Reporting Tools (BIRT) is a reporting technology that delivers formatted business data to printers and screens. The technology produces sophisticated output in PDF or HTML format, including graphics, tables, charts, and graphs. The developer can sort and otherwise manipulate data from databases, variables, or Web services. For additional background details, see *http://www.eclipse.org/birt*.

A report produced with BIRT can include values submitted by the EGL program that drives the report-creation process. As the report is being created, the report also can include values returned from one of several EGL functions used as event handlers. For example, the technology might invoke one event handler at the start of the report, one event handler at the start of a predefined report group (such as the sales data for a single type of product), and another event handler at the end of the report.

BIRT reports are available for logic that runs under JSE or JEE.

EGL Text Reporting

EGL text reporting creates reports that deliver the output of sophisticated business processes when you need neither graphical content nor an HTML- or PDF-formatted deliverable. The benefit is speed at both development and run time.

Several details described for BIRT reporting also hold true for text reporting. A text report can include values submitted by the EGL program that drives the report-creation process; EGL functions can act as event handlers; and EGL text reporting is available for logic that runs under JSE or JEE.

Print forms

An EGL *print form* is a set of character-based fields that a program writes periodically to a printer, either directly or by way of a file. Print forms are available for COBOL programs, JSE applications, and JEE application clients.

Integration with Existing Code

Your company can integrate EGL-generated code with existing software. EGL-generated COBOL code can interact with *native* (non-generated) programs on the same platform, whether the platform is CICS, IBM i, IMS, or z/OS batch. Similarly, EGL-generated Java code can call local, native programs written in C, C++, or Java; and can call remote CICS, IBM i, or IMS programs.

EGL provides two additional ways to integrate EGL-generated and native Java code. First, EGL lets you access a native Java interface or class from within your EGL code. You're able to use EGL syntax to work with the Java-based logic.

Second, you can cause a native Java class to call an EGL-generated program. This kind of integration involves a *Java wrapper*, a set of Java classes that will be deployed with the native class. The Java wrapper acts as an intermediary between the externally created code and the EGL-generated program.

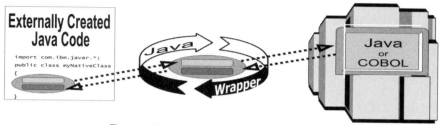

Figure 1.5: Use of a Java Wrapper at Run Time

As suggested in Figure 1.5, the EGL technology hides the details of data conversion. The native code invokes the Java wrapper, submitting data for transfer to the program. The wrapper then calls the program, which may be on a remote platform. The wrapper accepts the data returned from the program and relays the data back to the native code.

The Java wrapper is specific to the EGL-generated program being called, and the wrapper and program can be generated at the same time, as shown in Figure 1.6.

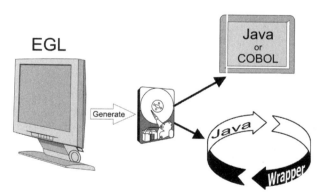

Figure 1.6: Generation of a Program and a Related Java Wrapper

Rational Business Developer and other Rational Products

You can use Rational Business Developer as a standalone product. Alternatively, RBD can be installed with any of the Eclipse-based products listed in this section. In either case, you work in a single, integrated development environment.

Here are the other products:

- *Rational Application Developer*

  An IDE for creating, testing, and deploying Java software, including Web applications, Enterprise JavaBeans (EJBs), and services.

  With this environent EGL developers can develop a *portal*, which is software that resides on a server and coordinates different user interfaces, each affecting a different area of a Web page. The output of a portal can provide a variety of news, business interaction, and entertainment.

  For details, see *http://www.ibm.com/software/awdtools/developer/application.*

- *Rational Developer for System z*

  An IDE for developing, testing, and deploying various kinds of code (assembler, C, C++, COBOL, and PL/I) for back-end z/OS environments, including UNIX System Services, CICS, and IMS. The product includes a seamless mechanism for working remotely on the z/OS-based code and datasets.

  For details, see *http://www.ibm.com/software/awdtools/devzseries.*

- *Rational Developer for System i*

  An IDE for developing, testing, and deploying COBOL and RPG for back-end IBM i environments. The product includes a seamless mechanism for working remotely on the IBM i-based code and datasets.

  For details, see *http://www.ibm.com/software/awdtools/rdi.*

- *Rational Developer for System i for SOA Construction*

  An IDE for developing Web or service-oriented solutions for the IBM i platform. The product combines the capabilites of Rational Business Developer and Rational Developer for System i.

For details, see
http://www.ibm.com/software/awdtools/rdisoa.

* *Rational Software Modeler*

An environment for designing applications. This product features the Unified Modeling Language (UML), which is an industry-standard language for modeling application structure and flow.

For details, see
http://www.ibm.com/software/awdtools/modeler/swmodeler.

* *Rational Software Architect*

An environment for designing and developing applications. This product combines the capabilities of Rational Application Developer and Rational Software Modeler and has tools for *Model Driven Development*, which is a technology for generating code from an application design.

For details, see
http://www.ibm.com/software/awdtools/architect/swarchitect.

* *Rational Data Architect*

An environment for designing and integrating data models and for ensuring that those models conform to an organization's standards. The product is especially useful when an organization has multiple databases that support applications in different departments. Rational Data Architect supports *logical models*, which are independent of a particular database management system (DBMS), and *physical models*, which are specific to a DBMS.

For details, see
http://www.ibm.com/software/data/integration/rda.

* *Rational Function Tester*

A tool for automating and running application tests, whether the applications are primarily involved in user interface or data access.

For details, see
http://www.ibm.com/software/awdtools/tester/functional.

- *Rational ClearCase®*

  A configuration management tool used by development teams. The tool maintains versions of the team's code, which may be stored on a variety of platforms, and provides ways to automate application builds and resolve coding conflicts.

  For details, see
  http://www.ibm.com/software/awdtools/clearcase.

- *Rational ClearQuest*

  A change management tool used by development teams. The tool tracks code defects, automates workflow, and helps ensure compliance with development processes and corporate regulations.

  For details, see
  http://www.ibm.com/software/awdtools/clearquest.

- *Rational Build Forge®*

  A tool for automating software builds, optionally with Rational ClearCase; and for managing product releases, including the application code, the installation code, and the legal detail.

  For details, see
  http://www.ibm.com/software/awdtools/buildforge.

Each product is built on the Eclipse environment, with product version 7.1 built on Eclipse 3.2.

CHAPTER 2

Overview of Generation

"Any sufficiently advanced technology is indistinguishable from magic."

Arthur C. Clarke

In this chapter, we describe the generation process. Our intent is to make you more comfortable with aspects of the RBD workbench and to give you insight into how your EGL code fits into a larger context.

EGL Compilation

As you develop EGL source code in the RBD workbench, the interface responds to your changes. For example, the EGL editor signals an error if you write an invalid function. After you fix the error, the name of the function is immediately displayed in the RBD **Outline** view, as shown in Figure 2.1.

How does the workbench respond to your code, signaling errors in the EGL editor and suddenly displaying data in a different view? Those behaviors are made possible by hidden EGL compilations, which convert your source code to an internal format of a kind later used as input to the EGL generator.

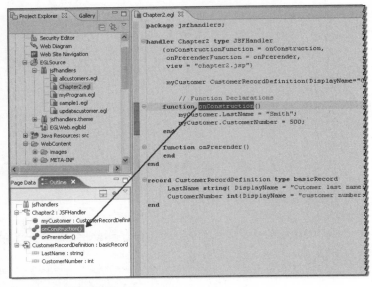

Figure 2.1: RBD Outline View

Each compilation validates whether the syntax of the source code is correct. The validation lets the RBD workbench respond interactively to syntax errors but does not catch errors that are specific to a target platform.

The *EGL compiler* is the system code that compiles your source code.

EGL Build

An *EGL build* is a process that compiles your EGL source-code files and stores the output in a set of files that are used for debugging and generation. The built files are called IR files because they provide an *intermediate representation* of the generated output (Figure 2.2).

Figure 2.2: EGL Build

By default, RBD performs an EGL build automatically each time you save your EGL source code. We suggest you accept the default behavior. If you don't re-create the IR files each time you save the EGL files, you may accidentally use old EGL source code when debugging the code or when generating output.

Most builds are incremental, adding content to existing IR files. The RBD workbench also provides the **Clean** option, which removes and rebuilds the IR files.

EGL Generation

An *EGL generation* is a process that requires not only IR files, but a set of rules that are specific to the target platform. Before generation, you provide those rules by specifying a set of definitions that are called *build parts*. The build parts affect how output is generated, as well as how output is built at deployment time.

The most important build part is the *build descriptor*, which identifies the target platform and that references other build parts as appropriate (Figure 2.3).

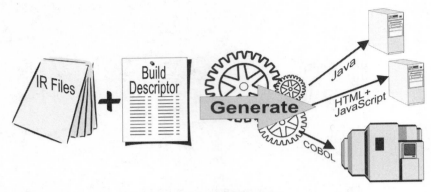

Figure 2.3: EGL Generation

EGL generation includes a second validation step to ensure that the input to generation is appropriate to the target platform. This validation step is the source of most messages from the EGL generator.

In regard to EGL generation, we suggest that you accept the RBD default behavior, which is to avoid the automatic generation of output after each build. In most cases, your development task is to repeatedly write, build, and debug, leaving generation for later in the process. Note that the default behavior of RBD includes some exceptions; for example, for JSF handler development. The exceptions are in effect when the debugging environment requires not only IR files and a build descriptor, but the generated output.

CHAPTER **3**

Language Organization

EGL has characteristics of Java and COBOL and includes innovations all its own. This chapter outlines how the language organizes data, logic, and presentation.

Data Types

In the broadest sense, a *data type*—for example, integer or string—defines a set of values and a set of operations that can act on those values. You can add two integers, each of which has a numeric range, or concatenate two strings, each of which has characters that are found in a particular set. The number 65 is said to be "of the type" integer.

As a developer, you associate digital values with data types (Figure 3.1).

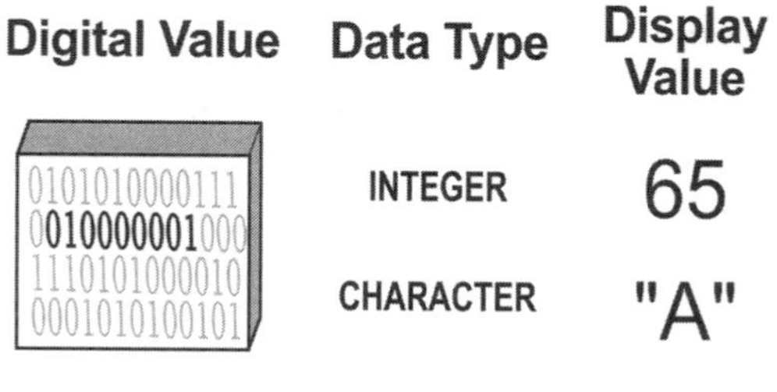

Digital Value	Data Type	Display Value
0101010000111 0010000001000 1110101000010 0001010100101	INTEGER	65
	CHARACTER	"A"

Figure 3.1: Digital Value and Display Value

A variable or constant is a name that refers to an area of memory. In EGL, the variable or constant is said to be *based on* a type, meaning that the value in the area is of the specified type.

EGL provides you with a set of primitive types—for example, STRING and INT (for integer)—and lets you create complex types. Each complex type is subdivided into fields, and any value based on a complex type is subdivided into fields as well.

An *instance* is a value to which you've applied a type. The type is a model of format, much as a blueprint is a model of a house (Figure 3.2).

Type   Instance

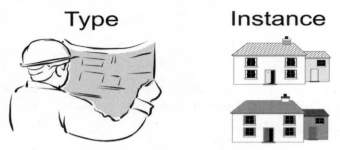

Figure 3.2: Type and Instance

Let's assume that you define the type **My_Customer_Record_Definition** to include the field **LastName**, which is of type STRING, and the field **CustomerNumber**, which is of type INT. Here's the EGL syntax.

```
Record My_Customer_Record_Definition
    LastName STRING;
    CustomerNumber INT;
end
```

A variable of type **My_Customer_Record_Definition** itself has a name (for example, myCustomer) and includes a customer name and number. Here's a variable declaration and field assignments.

```
myCustomer My_Customer_Record_Definition;

myCustomer.LastName = "Smith";
myCustomer.CustomerNumber = 500;
```

In EGL, the values of most types—for example, the field values "Smith" and 500—are available at business-application run time. You can also provide *annotations*, which are values that give direction to the EGL compiler or generator prior to run time.

Categories of EGL Data Types

The simplest EGL data types are called *primitive types*. Categories include numeric types; character types; date/time types, including timestamps (instances in time) and intervals (durations); large-object types (for memos, graphics, multimedia, and so on); and a single logic type, BOOLEAN.

The other data types are called *data parts*. The most elemental of these is the *DataItem part*, or more simply, a *data item*, which assigns a business-specific name in place of a primitive-type name. For example, a data item might assign the name **NumberOfCars** in place of INT.

A *Record part* lets you create a customized type that includes primitive types and data parts. Our example type **My_Customer_Record_Definition** was a Record part.

A *Dictionary part* offers storage and retrieval of entries at run time. The part allows you to write code that handles some advanced tasks in a more straightforward way than would be possible without the runtime flexibility.

EGL also offers a *DataTable part*, or more simply, a *data table*. This is a data collection in which you store, for example, a list of U.S. states and their postal abbreviations, often as part of a mechanism for validating user input. The data table is a *static part*, which means that the distinction between data type and variable is not meaningful because you use the part as needed, without declaring a variable.

Whenever the distinction between data type and variable *is* meaningful, you can create an array of elements of the type. A variable that is of type STRING array, for example, names a data area that addresses a series of elements, each of type STRING. We describe arrays in Chapter 4.

Many organizations maintain a collection of data-type names and related details. That collection is traditionally called a *data dictionary*, and it helps ensure that one program or service is accessible to another. The two kinds of EGL data types that are most appropriate for a data dictionary are data items and Record parts.

Data Item

Here's the definition for the data item **NumberOfCars**.

```
DataItem NumberOfCars INT end
```

The definition assigns a name that you can use instead of a primitive-type name such as INT. If you assign a name that is meaningful in a business sense, the data item provides clarity.

For example, the following code first declares a variable for the number of cars in an insurance policy and then assigns a value.

```
myCarCount NumberOfCars;
myCarCount = 2;
```

The effect at run time is the same as if you had declared a variable of type INT.

```
myCarCount INT;
myCarCount = 2;
```

Figure 3.3 illustrates the runtime equivalence.

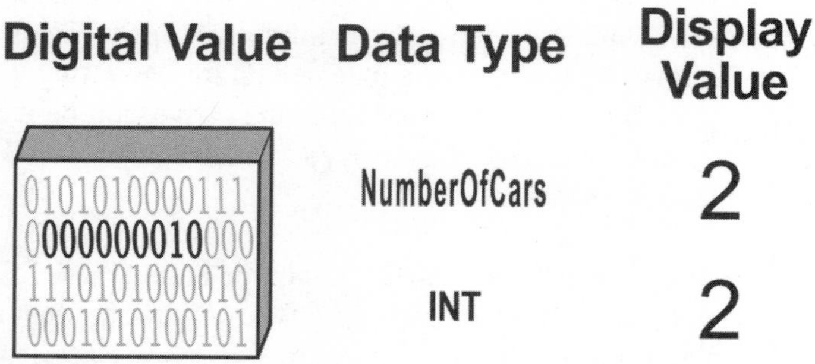

Figure 3.3: Equivalence of NumberOfCars and INT at Run Time

Your use of a data item helps you to focus on a business issue, and those who maintain your code gain the same benefit. And if the name reflects your organization's usual vocabulary, you gain the efficiency that comes from better communication among developers, Web designers, and business analysts.

Record Part

Business processing often requires you to create a sequence of fields that are processed as a unit. A *Record part* defines such a sequence. Here's an example.

```
Record CarPolicy type BasicRecord
    policyID STRING;
    carCount NumberOfCars;
    driverCount NumberOfDrivers;
end
```

The part has a name—in this case, **CarPolicy**—as well a list of fields. Each field is a declaration that includes a name, data type, and semicolon. The part is a model of format and is used for declaring a *record*, which is a variable that's based on the Record part. For example, here's a record declaration and subsequent record-field assignments.

```
myCarPolicy CarPolicy;

myCarPolicy.policyID = "ABC123";
myCarPolicy.carCount = 2;
```

Record Stereotypes

The use of the word *type* in the Record part can be misleading. Here, the word means *kind* and not a model of runtime format.

We'll work with the following kinds of Record parts in this book:

- **BasicRecord**. Records of this kind are for general processing, but not for input/output (I/O) against an external file or database.

- **SQLRecord**. Records of this kind are for exchanging data with a relational database.

- **Exception**. Records of this kind are for error handling.

Several other kinds of Record parts are available. A record based on a particular kind of part can exchange data with a particular kind of data storage such as sequential files, indexed files, and message queues.

The different kinds of Record parts provide our first example of a pattern we'll see again. A "type" category includes different kinds. For example, the Record part category includes SQLRecord and Exception kinds of Record parts. Each kind has a distinct syntax and a distinct business or technical purpose.

The technical term for "kind," in the sense described here, is *stereotype*. The distinction between EGL stereotypes such as SQLRecord and Exception is not that records of the two kinds have a different format at run time. The distinction is that records of the two kinds are processed differently by the EGL system code.

The notion of stereotypes comes from the Unified Modeling Language (UML), which is a graphical language used for business-process modeling and other purposes. Potentially, UML diagrams that reference EGL stereotypes can be an input to an automated process that creates EGL source code. The creation of source code from business models is generally described as Model Driven Development (MDD), and our use of the term *stereotype* points to the potential use of EGL in MDD.

Structured and Non-Structured Records

In addition to distinguishing Record parts as BasicRecord, SQLRecord, and so on, EGL distinguishes Record parts as *structured* or *non-structured*. Our previous examples represented the non-structured variation, which is useful for general processing and for accessing relational databases.

When you create a record based on a non-structured Record part, some fields in the record can reference areas that grow or shrink in size at run time. A field of type STRING, for example, might reference an area that contains the word *sedan* at one moment or the phrase *sports car* at another.

In contrast, a structured Record part is required when you need a specific runtime order of fixed-length fields. A record that's based on a structured Record part can act in several ways: accessing a file whose every field has a known, fixed length; transfering fixed-length data to or from another program; or accessing a DL/I database.

A field in a structured Record part can be based only on a type that provides a fixed length. For example, a field of type STRING is not valid; but a field of type CHAR(*size*) is, where *size* is the actual number of characters in the field.

If you create a field of type CHAR(6) and assign *sedan*, the field size remains the same, with a blank added after the last letter. If you later assign *sports car*, the field size remains the same, and the extra characters are truncated, leaving *sports*.

When you define a structured record part, you can assign level numbers to indicate a complex structure. Here's an example:

```
Record PersonPart type BasicRecord
    05 name CHAR(30);
        10 lastName CHAR(15);
        10 firstName CHAR(15);
    05 Address CHAR(51);
        10 line01 CHAR(15);
        10 line02 CHAR(15);
        10 city CHAR(10);
        10 stateCode CHAR(2);
        10 zip CHAR(9);
            15 zip5 CHAR(5);
            15 zipExtension CHAR(4);
    end
```

The use of level numbers lets you reference a sub-field by name. To set the sub-field **city** to the value *Boston*, for example, write the following variable declaration and assignment statement:

```
personVar PersonPart;
personVar.address.city = "Boston";
```

Although the maximum length of a structured record is fixed, your code can decide, at run time, to exclude the last fields in some situations. Those situations don't apply to any of the Record parts described elsewhere in this book; but we'll give you an idea of the capability without specifying every detail. Here's an example part.

```
Record PersonPart02 type SerialRecord
    { filename = "myLogicalFileName",
      numElementsItem = numberOfDegrees }
    05 name CHAR(30);
        10 lastName CHAR(15);
        10 firstName CHAR(15);
    05 numberOfDegrees SMALLINT;
    05 degrees[5]
        10 year SMALLINT;
        10 degree CHAR(10);
        10 school CHAR(20);
end
```

A record of type **PersonPart02** might include from zero to five educational degrees. The exclusion of some of the degree-related entries is possible when your code writes data from the record into a file and in other cases.

Dictionary Part

Unlike the data parts we've described so far, the Dictionary part is predefined and in that sense is like a primitive type. The purpose of the part is to declare a variable—a *dictionary*—to store and retrieve data whose identifier may be known only at run time.

As you work with a dictionary, you include *dictionary entries* such as those shown in the following variable declaration.

```
stockPrices Dictionary
{
    IBM = 165.25,
    GE  =  52.75
};
```

Each entry is composed of two components: a key (such as **IBM**) that lets you access a business value, and the business value itself. The entry can accommodate any type of value, and the values across entries can represent different types of data.

Once you've declared a dictionary, you can add, change, and delete entries; retrieve the keys and values; determine the number of entries in the dictionary; and test whether a given key is present.

Our example includes entry details that were set at development time. At run time, you can use data retrieved from whatever source as a key. For instance, you can create an application that retrieves stock symbols from the user and can organize the input in a dictionary, where each key is a different stock symbol.

After you retrieve an entry, you are likely to assign it to a variable of an appropriate type. The following example is possible if you know the type of data that was retrieved.

```
price DECIMAL(5,2);
price = stockPrices.IBM;
```

However, you may have stored several kinds of entries in a single dictionary at run time. For example, some value might be of a numeric type, for holding the price of a common stock; and some values might be based on a Record part, for holding the details of a stock option. After retrieving a value, you can use the operator **isa** to test the type of the value so as to ensure that subsequent processing is appropriate to the type. The operator **isa** returns a Boolean; in the following case, *true*.

```
if (stockPrices.IBM isa DECIMAL(5,2))
    ;
end
```

A real-world stock-quote application would use a bracket syntax, as described in Chapter 4. For now, we'll show you an example that's equivalent to the previous one.

```
mySymbol STRING = "IBM";
if (stockPrices[mySymbol] isa DECIMAL(5,2))
    ;
end
```

Data table

A *data table* is a data collection that other EGL code can access. Here's an example.

```
DataTable myErrorMessages type MsgTable
  msgNum INT;
  msgText char(30);

  { contents = [ [ 101, "File not found" ] ,
                 [ 102, "Read error" ] ,
                 [ 103, "Write error" ] ]
  }
end
```

As shown, the data table has a name, *myErrorMessages*. and a stereotype such as **MsgTable**. Next, variables indicate the type of data in every row; in this case, two columns are in use, one of type INT and one with as many as 30 characters. Last, a set-value block includes the value of the **contents** field, which is an array of arrays of type STRING.

Each inner array such as *101, "File not found"* holds the initial data for a row of the data table.

The following data-table stereotypes are available:

- **BasicTable**. A data table of this kind is for general processing; for example, a list of U.S. states and their postal abbreviations

- **MsgTable**. A data table of this kind contains runtime messages.

- **MatchValidTable**, **MatchInvalidTable**, or **RangeChkTable**. A data table of any of these kinds helps validate user input to a Web-page field or other onscreen field. In the first case (MatchValidTable), the input must match a value in the first data-table column. In the second case (MatchInvalidTable), the input must be different from any value in the first data-table column. In the third case (RangeChkTable), the input must match a value between the first and second column of at least one data-table row. If a validation fails, EGL displays an error message.

The data table is *generatable*, which means that you can request code to be generated by acting on the file that contains the part; for example, by right-clicking the file in the Rational Business Developer workbench and selecting **Generate**. The output created for a generated part is a standalone unit such as a program or binary file.

A data table is different from a dictionary in several ways, as outlined in Table 3-1.

Table 3-1: Comparison of Data Table and Dictionary		
	Data Table	**Dictionary**
Kinds of Data	Fixed length	Any kind of data
Number of Columns	Any number	Two
Number of Rows	Set before run time	May vary at run time
Validations	Special support	No special support

A data table can handle only fixed-length data, as was described in relation to structured records. A dictionary can handle any kind of data. A data table can have multiple columns. A dictionary can be used as a table, but only as a two-column table. You set the number of rows in a data table at development time. You can vary the number of entries in a dictionary at run time. Last, several kinds of data tables are helpful for validation, and EGL provides special support so that you can easily use data tables for that purpose. The language does not provide special support for dictionary-based validation.

Logic Parts

EGL includes a variety of *logic parts*, which process data. All have the following characteristics:

- Each logic part includes a set of functions. Each function is composed of EGL statements such as assignments, as well as identifiers— variables and constants—that are *local*: available only to the statements inside the function.

- Each logic part includes a set of identifiers that are at least *program global*: available to statements in every function in the part.

- Each logic part is generatable.

Consider the following logic part, a program that resides in the file MyProgram.egl.

```
program MyProgram

    const GREETING string = "Hello, ";
    suffix string;

    Function main()
        myName string = "Dave";
        suffix = "!!";
        SayHello(myName);
    end

    function SayHello(name string IN)
        sysLib.writeStdOut(GREETING + name + suffix);
    end
end
```

The function **main** runs first in any program. In this example, main assigns content to two variables and invokes the function **SayHello**. There, the plus sign (+) concatenates three strings. A system function, **sysLib.writeStdOut**, writes the text to the standard output, which is a file or display area that is specific to the runtime operating system. If you run a program in Rational Business Developer, the standard output is the Console view.

The output string is "Hello, Dave!!"

As used in any of the logic parts, a function can return a value of a specified type; and can include parameters, each corresponding to an argument in the function invocation. Each parameter includes a modifier, whether explicitly or by default:

- When the modifier is **IN** (the default), the parameter receives a value from the invoker, and the invoker does not receive any changes made to the parameter.

- When the modifier is **OUT**, the parameter gains an initial value according to initialization rules. For example, a parameter of type STRING has an initial value of spaces. When the function updates the parameter, the corresponding argument is updated in the invoker.

- When the modifier is **INOUT**, the parameter receives a value from the invoker and updates the argument when updating the parameter. If the argument is a constant such as the string "Smith," the behavior is the same as when the modifier is **IN**.

Categories of EGL Logic Parts

The EGL logic parts include *programs*, which define logic that starts at the same statement in every situation; *libraries*, which give local EGL code access to functions and data areas that are treated as part of the running code; *services*, which contain functions that can be accessed—possibly remotely—from other code; and *handlers*, which define a series of interactions that are specific to a runtime technology such as JSF or BIRT reports.

In some cases, EGL logic parts—and other parts we'll describe later—can be models of format. For example, to access a function in a service that you created, you might write code similar to the incomplete code shown here.

```
myService myServicePart;
myEmployee STRING = myService.getEmployee("910");
```

In this example, you declare a variable that's based on a Service part and use the variable to access a function coded in the part. The general rule is as follows: when a part is a model of format, the related variable provides access to data, logic, or both. The specific capability depends on the kind of part.

Program Within a Run Unit

A *program* always starts running at the same logical statement; in other words, has a single entry point. A *main program* is invoked by an operating-system command; by a transfer from another main program, in which case the transferring program ends; or by the function **vgLib.startTransaction**, in which case the invoking program continues running. A *called program* is invoked from a main or called program, and the caller waits for the called program to return control.

A called program can include parameters, which are program global. If the caller passes a variable, any change made to the corresponding parameter is available to the caller when the caller receives control again; and that rule applies even if one of the programs is written in a language other than EGL.

A *run unit* is not a logic part, but a collection of runtime software that works together such that a severe error in any of the code causes the operating system to remove all the code from memory. A main program and any program it calls, for example, are always in the same run unit and therefore share runtime properties, which assign resources such as files and database connections.

The details of what constitutes a run unit vary by platform.

Library

A *library* contains functions, variables, and constants that can be accessed from other EGL code running on the same platform. Each variable or constant that's external to any function is *run-unit global*, which means that the identifier is specific to a run unit and is available throughout the run unit. Each function is a separate entry point and, in a sense, so is each of the global identifiers, with an exception mentioned later.

Here's an example of a library, including two constants and a function.

```
library myLibrary type BasicLibrary {}

    const PREFIX STRING = "A1";
    const MINIMUM_BONUS BIN(9,2) = 100.00;

    // Function Declarations
    function getEmployee(employeeCode STRING) returns (STRING)
        if (employeeCode == "011")
            return (PREFIX + employeeCode);
        else
            return (employeeCode);
        end
    end
end
```

You can explicitly declare a library function, variable, or constant to be *private*, which means that the identifier can be accessed only from within the library. In the previous example, the constant named PREFIX could have been declared to be private.

```
private const PREFIX STRING = "A1";
```

Here's an example of a program that accesses the previous library and writes the string "A1011".

```
Program myProgram

    use myLibrary;

    Function main()
        myEmployee STRING = getEmployee("011");
        sysLib.writeStdOut(myEmployee);
    end
end
```

The program includes a **use** statement, which lets you reference names from the library as if they were local to the program. We'll revisit the **use** statement later.

Service

A *service* contains public functions that can be accessed from other code, potentially from anywhere in the world. The service can include private functions and global variables, but those functions and variables are solely for use by functions that are within the service.

At run time, a service written in EGL is *stateless*, which means that the internal logic never relies on data from a previous invocation. For example, a stock-quote service receives a trading symbol and returns a quote, and the data used in one invocation is independent of the data used in the next. In contrast, the variables in a library retain their values in a given run unit.

Here's an example of a service:

```
service myServicePart

    const PREFIX STRING = "001";
    const MINIMUM_BONUS BIN(9,2) = 100.00;

    // Function Declarations
    Function getEmployee(employeeCode STRING) returns (STRING)
        if (employeeCode == "910")
            return (PREFIX + employeeCode);
        else
            return (PREFIX);
        end
    end

    Function getMinimumBonus() returns (BIN (9,2))
        return(MINIMUM_BONUS);
    end
end
```

Additional details are needed to access the service at run time; first, to identify the *transport protocol*, which is software that oversees the runtime transmission of data to and from the service, and second, to identify the service location. The details are stored in a file named the *EGL deployment descriptor*. In many cases, you accept the values that are provided for you. A deployer can update the location details at deployment time.

Here's an example of a program that accesses a service.

```
Program myProgram

    Function main()
        myService myServicePart
            {
                @BindService
                    {bindingKey = "myServicePart"}
            };
        myEmployee STRING = myService.getEmployee("910");
        sysLib.writeStdOut(myEmployee);
    end
end
```

The example declares a variable based on the previously described service part, invokes the function getEmployee, and writes the string "001910".

The declaration of **myService** includes the annotation **BindService**, which identifies a *service client binding*. The service client binding details how the program accesses the service. In the example, the binding is named **myServicePart**. You must specify the **BindService** annotation, but if you don't specify the **bindingKey** field, the name of the binding is assumed to be the name of the Service part. The following declaration is also valid.

```
myService myServicePart { @BindService{} };
```

The service client binding is stored in the *program's* EGL deployment descriptor.

Any technique for working with a service is a variation on what we've shown here: create a variable, bind it to a service client binding, and access a function by way of the variable. Advanced techniques involve variables that are based on Interface parts, which we describe later.

Handler

A *handler* is code that defines a series of potentially complex interactions with the user. Handlers guide the behaviors of Rich UI applications, of Web pages that run under the JSF runtime, and of business reports written either with BIRT or with EGL text reporting.

We'll explore handlers in Chapter 7.

Prototype Parts

The word *prototype* reflects its use in C++, where a *function prototype*—the function name, parameters, and return type—includes the details needed to access a function but does not contain the function. Similarly, each EGL prototype part includes the details needed to access a particular kind of logic but does not contain the logic itself, which is defined elsewhere.

Categories of EGL Prototype Parts

The EGL prototype parts include *Interface parts*, which identify operations in a service; *external types*, which provide access to non-EGL code from within your code; and *Delegate parts*, which provide an advanced capability like that of function pointers in other languages. Each is of these parts is similar to a data part and is intended to be used as the basis of a variable.

Interface Part

An *Interface part* includes function prototypes that describe the operations in a service. Here's an example.

```
Interface MyInterface
    Function getEmployee(employeeCode STRING IN)
        returns (STRING);
    end
    Function getMinimumBonus()
        returns (BIN (9,2))
    end
end
```

The Interface part has two purposes. First, your organization can use the part as a tool for design. In this usage, a designer specifies a part that describes the service. You then code the service, which is said to *implement the interface*. The service contains every function described in the Interface part, which provides a kind of contract that the service must fulfill.

Second, the Interface part lets you access a service whose logic is not available. The lack of availability may result from the service being outside your company. For example, a business partner can deploy a remote Web service and make the interface details available. Those details are usually in the form of a Web Services Description Language (WSDL) file, which RBD can convert into an Interface part.

The lack of availability also might result from a decision. The service provider (your company or another) may want you to access the service by way of a variable that's based on the Interface part. Use of the part lets the provider avoid disclosing details of the service logic, either for competitive reasons or to reduce complexity. In either case, your focus is on the functionality that the service provides rather than on details that are internal to the service.

Here's an example of code that includes a variable based on an EGL Interface part.

```
Program myProgram

    Function main()
        myInterface myInterfacePart
            {
                @BindService
                    {bindingKey = "myInterfacePart"}
            };
        myEmployee STRING = myInterface.getEmployee("910");
        sysLib.writeStdOut(myEmployee);
    end
end
```

The variable provides access to the service. As shown, the declaration and access syntax are the same as in an earlier example, when we used a variable based on a Service part.

ExternalType Part

An *ExternalType* part, or *external type*, gives you a way to interact with non-EGL code from within your EGL logic. Two stereotypes are available. You can use a **JavaObject** stereotype to access or create Java code. And you can use a **JavaScriptObject** stereotype to access native JavaScript from a Rich UI application; in this way, you can use existing widget libraries such as Dojo and Silverlight when creating a user interface.

Delegate Part

A *Delegate part* provides an advanced capability. The part is the basis of a variable that lets you write code to invoke a *kind* of function—a function that has a given prototype. The variable lets you defer, until run time, the decision as to which function to invoke. The capability is used in applications that handle events. For example, when you develop a Web application, you might specify an EGL function to validate a user's input to a Web-page field. In that case, you are specifying a value that's based on a Delegate part, although the part is hidden from you.

To illustrate the general capability, we'll define **Responder**, a Delegate part.

```
Delegate Responder
   (howOld INT) returns (STRING)
end
```

Responder describes a function that accepts an integer (the age of a car, in years) and returns a string (the message to be displayed after a user's request for an insurance quote is processed).

Here's **Responder**, along with a program that uses it.

```
Delegate Responder
   (howOld INT) returns (STRING)
end

Program ProcessQuote(VIN STRING)

  Function AntiqueCarQuote(howManyYears INT) returns (STRING)
    return ("We can insure your antique!");
  end

  Function RecentCarQuote(thisOld INT) returns (STRING)
   return ("We can insure your car!");
  end

  Function main()
    response Responder;
    message STRING;
    age INT = 30;

   if (age >= 25)
      response = AntiqueCarQuote;
    else
      response = RecentCarQuote;
    end

    message = response(age);
    sysLib.WriteStdOut(message);
  end
end
```

Listing 3.1: Delegate part

The program **ProcessQuote** itself accepts a string (**VIN**, the Vehicle Identification Number) and includes two functions other than **main**. Both of those functions have the same prototype as the function described in the Delegate part.

Three declarations are in the function **main**: one for **response**, a variable based on the Delegate part; one for **message**, a string to display; and one for **age**, an integer that contains the car's age, which is set to 30 in this case. An **if** statement specifies which function to assign to **response**:

```
if (age >= 25)
   response = AntiqueCarQuote;
else
   response = RecentCarQuote;
end
```

Next, the variable **response** is used as if its name were the name of a function:

```
message = response(age);
```

Last, the EGL function **sysLib.writeStdOut** writes the value returned from the selected function.

```
sysLib.WriteStdOut(message);
```

The output from this example is "We can insure your antique!".

User Interface Parts

Some EGL parts fall into multiple categories. Handlers include logic and affect user interface; and the Console UI parts are external types that also affect user interface. For our purposes, EGL provides two user interface parts: *Form* and *Form Group*.

Form Part

A *Form part*—usually called a *form*—is a set of character-based fields that are organized for presentation. Like a data table, the form is a static part; it is not the basis of a variable, but is a data collection that other EGL code can access directly. You create the form with an editor in the RBD workbench.

Two kinds of forms are possible. A *text form* is a form displayed at a standalone terminal or in a workstation window. This type of form is used by a *textUI program*, which is a program whose only onscreen interaction is by way of these forms. In contrast, a *print form* is displayed by a printer—or in a text file—and is used by a library or by any kind of program. Each form has a fixed, internal structure like that of a structured record, but a form cannot include a substructure.

A form is available to a program or library only if the form is included in or referenced by a form group and only if the program or library identifies the form group in a **use** statement, which we describe later.

FormGroup part

A *FormGroup* part—usually called a *form group*—is a collection of text and print forms and is a generatable UI part. A program can include only one form group for most uses, along with one form group for help-related output. The same form can be included in multiple form groups.

Annotations

An *annotation* is a value that helps the EGL system code to set up an interaction with a runtime technology. Annotations are available only to the EGL compiler and generator, not to the statements in your runtime code.

You specify annotations for various reasons. In one case, you set a database-table name that's embedded in the generated code. In another case, you identify the function to invoke when a user clicks a Web-page button. In a third case, you set the output file name for an EGL-generated program.

Let's look at that last case, which involves the **Alias** annotation. The effect of **Alias** is to help set the name of an output file. The annotation is most useful if you're generating code for an environment that supports only short names. For the Java output emphasized in this book, the following source code ensures that a generated program is named **MyProg.java**.

```
Program AnExtraordinaryProgram { Alias = "MyProg" }

end
```

We'll explain the syntax in a moment, but want to emphasize that an annotation is "of a type"; and the type is always a Record part such as the one shown here.

```
Record Alias type Annotation
   value STRING;
end
```

When you think about an annotation that has only one field, you may find yourself talking about the annotation field as if it were the annotation. For example, you might say that the **Alias** annotation is of type STRING. As EGL moves toward letting developers extend the language, we'd like the underlying detail to be understood. The annotation is never of a primitive type. The annotation is based on a Record part. In this case, the annotation is of type Alias, and an annotation field in that Record part is of type STRING.

Note: The RBD product documentation uses two phrases that are equivalent to annotation field: *property field* and *simple property.*

Annotation Syntax

You can further refine the purpose of a data item by specifying various annotations; for example, **DisplayName** and **InputRequired**.

```
DataItem
    NumberOfCars INT
    { DisplayName = "Number of Cars",
      InputRequired = yes }
end
```

Any annotation in a data item represents a default characteristic that pertains to any variable that is based on the data item. In this case, if a Web-page field is based on **NumberOfCars**, the defaults are as follows: the label "Number of Cars" is on the page, adjacent to the field, and the user is required to enter data.

The annotations that are available for primitive types or data items are called *field-level annotations*. To specify those annotations, you code a *set-value block*, which is an area of code between opening and closing braces. As shown, one annotation is separated from the next by a comma. The *target* of the set-value block is the language element that is affected by the entries in the set-value block. In this case, the target is the data item being defined. The target precedes the set-value block.

The syntax of the previous example is so concise that it may mislead you. The following syntax communicates the relationships more clearly.

```
DataItem
    NumberOfCars INT
    { @DisplayName { value = "Number of Cars"},
      @InputRequired { value = yes } }
end
```

The at sign (@) directs the EGL system code to create a new annotation of the specified type, whether the type is **DisplayName** or **InputRequired**. The embedded set-value block lists all the field-value pairs for the new annotation.

Whenever an annotation type has exactly one field, you can create a new annotation with syntax such as **DisplayName = "Number of Cars"**. You're assigning a value of the appropriate field type—in this case, STRING—and ignoring the name of the field.

Data Items and Variables

The annotations that are valid for any data items are valid for all data items. For instance, in our example, no error occurs if you declare a variable based on **NumberOfCars** and fail to use the variable as a Web-page field. The benefit of this rule is that you can use the same data item to declare several variables, each of which might be used in a different way. One variable of type **NumberOfCars** might be used for data storage, one for general processing, and one for data presentation.

The annotations specified for a data item represent a default that you can override when you declare a variable that's based on the data item. You can accept or override individual annotations from the default set, and you can add annotations from the set of field-level annotations. Here's an example of a variable declaration.

```
myCarCount NumberOfCars
    { DisplayName = "Quantity",
      InputRequiredMsgKey = "Message101" }
end
```

If the variable **myCarCount** is used on a Web-page field, the result is as follows: The label "Quantity" is on the page instead of "Number of Cars"; the user is required to enter data although no mention of that requirement is in the variable declaration; and a failure to place data will cause the display of a message that is referenced by the string "Message101", which is not mentioned in the data item at all.

You might describe your coding in the following way: you assign a business value like 2 *into* **myCarCount,** and you assign an annotation like DisplayName *onto* **myCarCount.**

Stereotypes

Earlier, we noted that the term *stereotype* in EGL refers to a kind of data type—for example, to a kind of Record part that makes your interaction with a relational database easier. Assume now that a systems architect want to use an EGL stereotype. What the architect seeks is a runtime behavior such as database access. The runtime behavior is affected by the processing of the EGL system code. In short, the architect seeks an annotation.

At the level of EGL source code, a stereotype is an annotation that specifies the extra detail needed to handle an instance of a complex type. For example, here's a Record part whose stereotype is SQLRecord and which defines a relationship with the relational-database table **Policy**.

```
Record CarPolicy type SQLRecord
   { tableNames =
        [["Policy"]],
     keyItems = [policyID] }
   policyID STRING;
   carCount NumberOfCars;
end
```

Here's a declaration of an instance.

```
myCarPolicy CarPolicy;
```

The stereotype SQLRecord identifies what must be done to process the instance.

Let's look more closely at the syntax used to set stereotypes. When we first described a set-value block, we showed a concise syntax that included the annotation name but ignored the annotation-field name. In the current example, **tableNames** and **keyItems** are stereotype-field names—and are therefore annotation-field names. The following definition is equivalent to the previous one.

```
Record CarPolicy
{ @SQLRecord
    { tableNames =
        [["Policy"]],
      keyItems =
        [policyID] }
    policyID STRING;
    carCount NumberOfCars;
end
```

The target of the outer set-value block is the Record part being defined. The at sign (@) directs the EGL system code to create a new annotation of the specified type; here, type SQLRecord. The embedded set-value block lists all the field-value pairs for the new annotation.

Set-Value Blocks

As shown earlier, you can use a set-value block to set annotations. You can also use set-value blocks to set values for run time. The next example assigns a default value to an SQL record field.

```
Record CarPolicy type SQLRecord
    { policyID = "9999",
      tableNames =
        [["Policy"]],
      keyItems = [policyID] }
    policyID STRING;
    carCount NumberOfCars;
end
```

In any record that's based on CarPolicy, the values of field **policyID** is "9999" by default. You can override a field default in the record declaration, as shown next.

```
myCarPolicy CarPolicy
    { policyID = "ABC123",
      carCount = 2 };
```

Here's another example of a set-value block: a dictionary, where you can set annotations such as **CaseSensitive** and entries such as IBM.

```
stockPrices Dictionary
{
    // annotation
    CaseSensitive = No,

    // dictionary entries
    IBM = 165.25,
    GE  =  52.75
}
```

That setting of **CaseSensitive** lets your code refer to the first dictionary entry as *IBM*, *IbM*, or *ibm*.

In some cases, you'll want to use a set-value block to refer to nested fields. Here is a record part that defines a relationship with a relational-database table named **PreferredPolicy**.

```
Record CarPolicyPreferred type SQLRecord
    { tableNames = [["PreferredPolicy"]],
      keyItems = [preferredID] }

    preferredID STRING;
    onePolicy CarPolicy;
    serviceLevel INT;
end
```

When you declare a variable of type **CarPolicyPreferred**, you can nest a set-value block to initialize the field **onePolicy**.

```
Program myProgram

    function main()
        policyVar CarPolicyPreferred
        { preferredID = "ABC123",
            onePolicy{ policyID = "ABC123", carCount = 2 },
            serviceLevel = 1 };
    end
end
```

As shown, the syntax involves preceding the nested set-value block with the name of the field whose own fields are being initialized.

You can nest set-value blocks to reference fields in records that are themselves nested, to any level of Icomplexity.

Packages

The EGL language organizes parts into *packages*. All code—including EGL system code—is in a package and can access all parts in the same package, even if the code is spread across different files.

In general, a package name is a sequence of identifiers separated by periods (.), as in this example: *com.myCompany.myCommonPkg*. Each name corresponds to a subfolder at development time and, for Java output, at deployment time. In this example, the directory structure includes the folder *com*, the subfolder *myCompany*, and the sub-subfolder *myCommonPkg*.

As a result of a collaboration or merger, your work may be combined with the work of another organization. To ensure that your package names are unique, you can make the initial part of a package name an inversion of your company's Internet domain name. If your company's domain name is *ibm.rational.software.com*, for example, your company's package names might start with *com.software.rational.ibm*.

The rules for specifying the lowest-level qualifiers in a package name vary from company to company, with different packages reflecting a difference between development groups, business purposes, runtime platforms, or some other characteristic of the business.

An EGL file in one package can access parts in a second. Consider, for example, a source file that holds the data item parts used in several applications:

```
package com.myCompany.myCommonPkg;

DataItem NumberOfDrivers INT end

DataItem NumberOfCars INT end
```

The package *com.myCompany.myCommonPkg* includes at least the two data item parts. Let's consider a second source file, which holds a Record part in the package *com.myCompany.myApplicationPkg*:

```
package com.myCompany.myApplicationPkg;

import com.myCompany.myCommonPkg.*;

Record CarPolicy type BasicRecord
  policyID CHAR(10);
  driverCount NumberOfDrivers;
  carCount NumberOfCars;
end
```

In general, an import statement *imports* (that is, makes available) one or more parts in a package. In such a statement, a period and asterisk (.*) at the end of a package name makes available every part in the package; and in the current example, the import statement makes available the data item parts shown earlier.

You can specify a part name instead of an asterisk. The effect is to make a single part available. The following code gives two examples:

```
package com.myCompany.myApplicationPkg;

import com.myCompany.myCommonPkg.NumberOfDrivers;
import com.myCompany.myCommonPkg.NumberOfVehicles;

Record CarPolicy type BasicRecord
  policyID CHAR(10);
  driverCount NumberOfDrivers;
  carCount NumberOfCars;
end
```

The next example shows that you can avoid specifying an import statement altogether:

```
package com.myCompany.myApplicationPkg;

Record CarPolicy type BasicRecord
  policyID CHAR(10);
  driverCount com.myCompany.myCommonPkg.NumberOfDrivers;
  carCount com.myCompany.myCommonPkg.NumberOfCars;
end
```

The parts **NumberOfDrivers** and **NumberOfCars** are available in this case because you've qualified each part name with the name of the package in which the part resides.

Two types or parts cannot have the same name in a given package. However, a given part name can appear in many different packages. When you create an application, you'll need to know the rules for identifying which part is referenced when you use a particular part name:

- If the name of a part is qualified by a package name (as in our example of **com.myCompany.myPkg.NumberOfDrivers**), EGL seeks the part in the specified package.

- If a part name is not qualified, EGL first reviews the single-part import statement, if any, that refers to the name; our example is **import com.myCompany.myPkg.NumberOfDrivers**. In a given source file, only one single-part import statement is valid for a given part name.

- If the part name is still not resolved, EGL checks the current package.

- If necessary, EGL reviews the parts in multiple-part import statements such as **import com.myCompany.myCommonPkg.***. An error occurs if two of those statements provide access to a same-named part.

- If necessary, EGL checks the EGL system scope; primarily to find one of the many EGL system functions or variables.

If you're working in the RBD workbench, the rules for resolving part names are affected by the *EGL build path*, which is a list of all projects whose parts can be accessed from your project. If you're generating code in the EGL

SDK, the rules are affected by the *eglpath*, which is a list of directories whose parts can be accessed when generating code in a batch process. Using projects in the workbench is similar to using eglpath directories, so for purposes of explanation we'll assume you're working with the EGL build path.

At each of the steps described earlier, EGL searches the current project; then, if necessary, searches the next project in the EGL build path; and then, if necessary, searches the next project. If a part name is resolved in a given project, the search ends.

You can create a source file that identifies no package name at all. In this case, the code resides in a *default package*, which is simply in a high-level folder. However, use of a default package is discouraged because other packages cannot access the parts in such a package.

Use Statement

In most cases, the **use** statement is a convenience that lets you easily reference variables, constants, and functions that are declared in libraries and other generatable parts. For example, assume that a library named **CustomerLib** is in your current package and includes the function **getCustomer**. The following is valid.

```
package com.myCompany.myPkg;

program myProgram type BasicProgram
    function main()
        CustomerLibrary.getCustomer();
    end
end
```

You can add a **use** statement to save you from having to qualify the referenced name. The following example is equivalent to the previous one.

```
package com.myCompany.myPkg;

program myProgram type BasicProgram

    use CustomerLibrary;

    function main()
        getCustomer();
    end
end
```

Depending on your declaration of **import** and **use** statements, a reference— for example, to **getCustomer**—may be qualified with a package name; with the package name, a dot, and the name of the generatable part; or with only the name of the generatable part. The simplest alternative is to have no qualifier and to reference only the variable, constant, or function in the generatable part.

CHAPTER 4

Runtime Values

The rules for working with data are an important aspect of EGL, and we cover the issue in detail.

Constants

A *constant* names an unchangeable data area. Here are some declarations.

```
const TOPSCORE, MAXVALUE, UPPER INT = 100;
const COPYSTRING STRING = "Copyright 2010";
const AGES INT[] = [5, 6, 7];
```

As shown, you declare a constant by specifying the symbol **const**, a name or a list of comma-separated names, a primitive type or array, and an assignment.

You use a constant as if it were the assigned literal. The name helps you to think about a business problem and lets you change every use of the constant by changing the one declaration.

Variables

A *variable* names a changeable data area. Here are some declarations.

```
policyID, counter, salesInQuarter INT;
copyright STRING;
salesByQuarter INT[];
```

As shown, you declare a varaible by specifying a name or a list of comma-separated names, followed by a type or array.

Two kinds of variables are available in EGL. A *value variable* names a data area containing a value of direct interest to your application. For example, a variable of type INT might name a data area that holds the number of items sold in a quarter (Figure 4.1).

salesInQuarter

Figure 4.1: Value Variable

In contrast, a *reference variable* names a data area containing a memory address. The address has no direct interest to your application, but refers to one or more data areas that do.

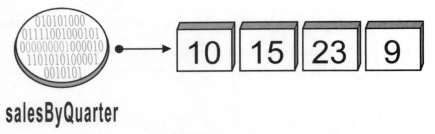

salesByQuarter

Figure 4.2:   Reference Varaible

In Figure 4.2, the variable **salesByQuarter** is of type INT array. The named data area in turn references a series of data areas that contain the number of items sold in each of the last four quarters.

Our description of the two kinds of variables doesn't fully express what occurs at run time, but accurately tells what you need to understand as you access data areas in your code.

Given a particular variable, is it a value variable or a reference variable? The
determining factor is the data type on which the variable is based (Table 4-1).

Table 4-1: Value and Reference Types		
	Value	**Reference**
Primitive Types and Related Data Items	All numeric, character, and datetime types, as well as BOOLEAN	ANY and the large-object types
Complex Types	Record parts other than Exception	Exception Record; External Type; Dictionary, Service, Interface, and Delegate parts; and Dynamic-array types

Most primitive types are value types, including STRING. Most Record parts are
value types, too, with the exception of... Exception.

The simplest reference types are ANY and the large-object types. Among the
other reference types are External Types and the following EGL parts:
Dictionary, Service, Interface, and Delegate. Also, dynamic array types—for
example, INT array—are reference types; and later we'll show how that fact
affects what happens when you copy arrays.

If your data structures get complicated, we suggest you draw simple diagrams
to reflect the relationships, with circles for the areas named by reference
variables and rectangles for the areas named by value variables, as shown in
this chapter.

In many cases, a value variable is initialized. For example, a global variable of
type BOOLEAN is set to *false* automatically. However, no initialization occurs
for a reference variable, and you must initialize the variable before you can
use it as a source of data. The phrase "to initialize a reference variable" means
to cause the variable to address a data area or, as shown later, to enable use of
the variable for function invocation.

When working with reference variables, you can use **null** to indicate explicitly that the variable is not initialized. Here's an example.

```
Program myProgram type BasicProgram

    Function main()
        myDictionary Dictionary = null;
    end
end
```

Using the New Operator

The **new** operator *allocates*—that is, reserves—a data area at run time and places the area's address into a variable. For example, the following code creates an area of type Dictionary, which is a reference type.

```
Program myProgram type BasicProgram

    Function main()
        myDictionary Dictionary = new Dictionary;
    end
end
```

You can use the **new** operator even if you're working with a value type. The following example creates an array of basic records.

```
Record MyCustomerType type BasicRecord
    ID INT;
    name STRING;
end
Program myProgram type BasicProgram

    Function main()
        myCustomers MyCustomerType[] = [
            new MyCustomerType
                { ID = 120, name = "IBM" },
            new MyCustomerType
                { ID = 121, name = "MC Press" }
        ];
        sysLib.writeStdOut (myCustomers[1].name);
    end
end
```

The code writes *IBM* to the standard output.

Using a Set-Value Block with a Reference Variable

You can initialize a reference variable without the **new** operator. In this case, you specify a set-value block in the variable declaration. Each statement in the next example allocates a new data area.

```
Program myProgram type BasicProgram

   Function main()
      myDictionary Dictionary{ };
      myDictionary02 Dictionary { x = 1, y = 2 };
   end
end
```

Specifying the set-value block with a reference variable is not always identical to using the **new** operator. You can use the set-value block to update the fields of an existing data area. Consider the next example.

```
Program myProgram type BasicProgram

   Function main()
      myDictionary Dictionary = null;
      myDictionary{ IBM = 100, GE = 40};
      myDictionary{ IBM = 125, GE = 45};
   end
end
```

The first statement in the function creates a reference variable that doesn't refer to a data area. The second statement allocates a data area, and the third statement reassigns values to the same data area. Consider the following variation.

```
Program myProgram type BasicProgram

   Function main()
      myDictionary Dictionary = null;
      myDictionary{ IBM = 100, GE = 40 };
      myDictionary = new Dictionary{ IBM = 125, GE = 45 };
   end
end
```

That last statement creates a new dictionary, and the area of memory to which **myDictionary** referred in the second statement is made available for other purposes, automatically.

Arrays

EGL supports array literals, dynamic arrays, and structure-field arrays. We'll look at each in turn.

Array Literals

An array literal consists of a pair of brackets enclosing either a comma-separated list of literals—including other array literals—or more complex expressions. Each array literal has a type and can be used anywhere an array of that type is allowed. The following example assigns an array literal of type INT to the reference variable **myArray**.

```
myArray INT[] = [1,2,3];
```

Table 4-2 shows other examples.

Table 4-2: Examples of Literal Arrays	
Array Literal	**Type**
["bye", "ciao"]	STRING[]
[(myPay < 10000), (yourPay > 50000)]	BOOLEAN[]
[[1, 2], [3, 4]]	SMALLINT[][] (a two-dimensional array)
[3, "ciao", 4.5, 6.7]	ANY[]

Dynamic Arrays

A dynamic array is an array whose number of elements is changeable at run time. This kind of array can be based on a primitive type, on a data part, or on a logic or prototype part used as a data part.

You make a size change by invoking an array-specific function such as **removeElement**, **insertElement**, or **appendElement**. Other functions let you increase or decrease the maximum number of elements allowed. However, you cannot invoke any function unless the array is initialized. The following declaration does not specify an initial number of elements but includes a set-value block, which fulfills the initialization requirement.

```
age INT[] {};
```

The following code declares a dynamic array of 3 elements, each of type INT.

```
age INT[3] { maxSize=5 };
```

The example includes the annotation **MaxSize**, which specifies the maximum number of elements. In this case, an attempt to add more than 5 elements to the array causes an exception at run time.

You can assign values to the array at declaration time, whether by assigning an array literal or by including the values in a set-value block.

```
age INT[5] = [27, 35, 29, 42, 53];
age INT[5]   {27, 35, 29, 42, 53};
```

Similarly, the following examples assign values to a multi-dimensional array; in this case, an array of 2 rows and 3 columns.

```
myTable INT[2][3] = [ [1, 2, 3], [4, 5, 6] ];
myTable INT[2][3]   { [1, 2, 3], [4, 5, 6] };
```

To reference an element, you use *array indexes*, expressions that resolve to integers and are used to identify the element. Here are examples; first, an array element being assigned to another variable, and second, a value being assigned to an array element.

```
// assign 29 to myAge
myAge INT = age[3];

// replace 2 with 12
myTable[1][2] = 12;
```

Structure-Field Arrays

You declare a structure-field array when you specify that a field in a
structured record has multiple occurrences, as in the following example.

```
Record ExampleRecord01
    10 myItem CHAR(1)[3];
end
```

If a structured record variable named **myRecord** is based on that definition,
the name **myRecord.myItem** refers to a one-dimensional array of three
elements, each a character, and you can reference the second element by
typing **myRecord.myItem[1]**.

Also, you can declare a structure-field array of multiple dimensions, as
shown next.

```
Record ExampleRecord02
    10 myArray[3];
        20 myEmbeddedArray CHAR(20)[2];
end
```

If a record variable named **myRecord02** is based on that definition, each
element of the one-dimensional array **myRecord02.myArray** is itself a one-
dimensional array; and you can refer to the second of the three subordinate
one-dimensional arrays as **myRecord02.myArray[2]**. The structure field
myEmbeddedArray declares a two-dimensional array, and the next example
demonstrates the preferred syntax for referring to an element of that array.

```
// for row 1, column 2
myRecord02.myArray[1].myEmbeddedArray[2]
```

Assigning One Variable to Another

In this section, we'll illustrate four kinds of assignments and use in-code comments to detail the effect. Table 4-3 gives a summary.

Table 4-3: Assigning One Variable to Another	
Kind of Assignment	**Effect**
Value to Value	Copies the value from the sender to the receiver
Value to Reference	Copies the value from the sender to a new area and causes the receiver to reference that area
Reference to Reference	Causes the receiver to reference the area that the sender was referencing already
Reference to Value	Copes the value from the referenced area to the receiver

This section also shows the practical implications; first, by assigning a customer-contact record that references a list of people at the customer site, and second, and by adding a similar record to an array of records, as might be necessary for contacting people at many customer sites. The array processing is particularly important.

Value Variable to a Value Variable

The assignment of a value variable, literal, or constant to a value variable is a straightforward copying of data from one area to another (Figure 4.3).

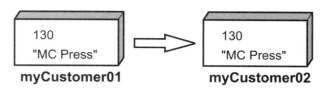

myCustomer01   **myCustomer02**

Figure 4.3: Assigning a Value Variable to a Value Variable

Value Variable to a Reference Variable

You can assign a value variable to a reference variable. In Figure 4.4 and in subsequent sections, the white arrow represents the assignment, the dotted arrow represents a physical copying of data, and the solid black arrow represents a reference.

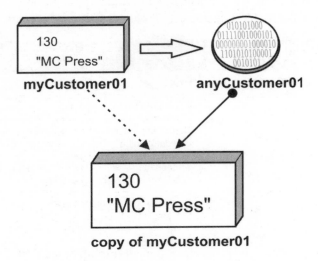

Figure 4.4: Assigning a Value Variable to a Reference Variable

The following code copies a value variable—in this case, a basic record—to a variable of type ANY.

```
Record MyCustomerType type BasicRecord
    ID INT;
    name STRING;
end

Program myProgram type BasicProgram
    Function main()
        myCustomer01 MyCustomerType;
        myCustomer01.ID = 130;
        myCustomer01.name = "MC Press";

        anyCustomer01 ANY = myCustomer01;
        anyCustomer01.name = "IBM";

        sysLib.writeStdOut(myCustomer01.ID);      // 130
        sysLib.writeStdOut(myCustomer01.name);    // MC Press
        sysLib.writeStdOut(anyCustomer01.ID);     // 130
        sysLib.writeStdOut(anyCustomer01.name);   // IBM
    end
end
```

Listing 4.1: Assigning a Value Variable to a Reference Variable

The assignment of **myCustomer01** to **anyCustomer01** does not copy the
address of **myCustomer01**. Instead, the assignment copies the content of
myCustomer01 to a separate data area, and causes **anyCustomer01** to refer to
that area. The assigment of *IBM* to **anyCustomer01.name** does not affect
myCustomer01.

Reference Variable to a Reference Variable

The next example begins with two operations that are equivalent to the one in
the previous section, when a value variable was assigned to a reference
variable. The inset in Figure 4.5 shows the situation that's in effect after the
two operations are complete.

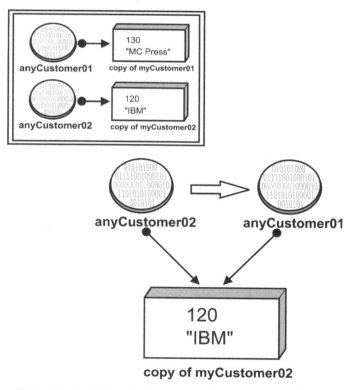

Figure 4.5: *Assigning a Reference Variable to a Reference Variable*

The center of Figure 4.5 shows that after one of the reference variables is
copied to the other, the two reference variables refer to the same data area.

Now consider the code. To fulfill the inset in Figure 4.5, we create two value variables—again, basic records—and assign them to variables of type ANY. To fulfill the center of Figure 4.5, we then copy one variable of type ANY to the other variable of type ANY.

```
Record MyCustomerType type BasicRecord
   ID INT;
   name STRING;
end

Program myProgram type BasicProgram

   Function main()
      myCustomer01, myCustomer02 MyCustomerType;
      myCustomer01.ID = 130;
      myCustomer01.name = "MC Press";
      myCustomer02.ID = 120;
      myCustomer02.name = "IBM";

      anyCustomer01 ANY = myCustomer01;
      anyCustomer02 ANY = myCustomer02;
      anyCustomer01 = anyCustomer02;
      anyCustomer01.ID = 100;

      sysLib.writeStdOut(myCustomer01.ID);     // 130
      sysLib.writeStdOut(myCustomer01.name);   // MC Press
      sysLib.writeStdOut(myCustomer02.ID);     // 120
      sysLib.writeStdOut(myCustomer02.name);   // IBM
      sysLib.writeStdOut(anyCustomer01.ID);    // 100
      sysLib.writeStdOut(anyCustomer01.name);  // IBM
      sysLib.writeStdOut(anyCustomer02.ID);    // 100
      sysLib.writeStdOut(anyCustomer02.name);  // IBM
   end
end
```

Listing 4.2: Assigning a Reference Variable to a Reference Variable

Again, each time a value variable such as **myCustomer02** is assigned to a reference variable such as **anyCustomer02**, the value variable is unaffected by the assignment. The reference variable addresses a copy of the values that were in the original data area.

The example assignment of **anyCustomer02** to **anyCustomer01** has two effects:

- The data area that previously held a copy of myCustomer01 is made available for other purposes, automatically.

- Both variables of type ANY now address the same data area, which holds a copy of **myCustomer02**. Assigning a value to a field in **anyCustomer01** changes a field that is referenced by both **anyCustomer01** and **anyCustomer02**.

You may want to copy data from one reference variable to another such that, after the operation ends, the two variables point to different data areas. The option is available if you use the EGL **move** statement (Figure 4.6).

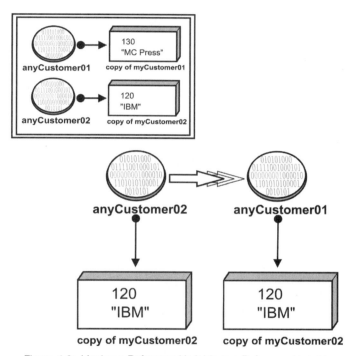

Figure 4.6: Moving a Reference Variable to a Reference Variable

The following example is similar to the previous one, but two boldfaced statements demonstrate the use and effect of a **move** statement in place of an assignment.

```
Record MyCustomerType type BasicRecord
    ID INT;
    name STRING;
end

Program myProgram type BasicProgram

    Function main()
        myCustomer01, myCustomer02 MyCustomerType;
        myCustomer01.ID = 130;
        myCustomer01.name = "MC Press";
        myCustomer02.ID = 120;
        myCustomer02.name = "IBM";

        anyCustomer01 ANY = myCustomer01;
        anyCustomer02 ANY = myCustomer02;
        // we replace this: anyCustomer01 = anyCustomer02;
        move anyCustomer02 to anyCustomer01;
        anyCustomer01.ID = 100;

        sysLib.writeStdOut(myCustomer01.ID);     // 130
        sysLib.writeStdOut(myCustomer01.name);   // MC Press
        sysLib.writeStdOut(myCustomer02.ID);     // 120
        sysLib.writeStdOut(myCustomer02.name);   // IBM
        sysLib.writeStdOut(anyCustomer01.ID);    // 100
        sysLib.writeStdOut(anyCustomer01.name);  // IBM
        sysLib.writeStdOut(anyCustomer02.ID);    // 120
        sysLib.writeStdOut(anyCustomer02.name);  // IBM
    end
end
```

Listing 4.3: One Use of the Move Statement

Reference Variable to a Value Variable

The next example begins with an operation equivalent to an earlier one, when a value variable was assigned to a reference variable. The inset in Figure 4.7 shows the situation that's in effect after the operation is complete.

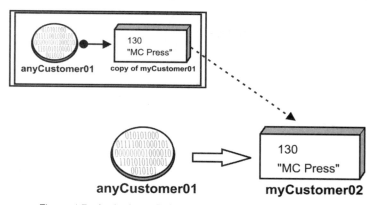

Figure 4.7: Assigning a Reference Variable to a Value Variable

The center of Figure 4.7 shows the effect of assigning a reference variable to a value variable: the value of the referenced data area is copied to the value variable.

Now consider the code. To fulfill the inset in Figure 4.7 we create a value variable—a basic record—and assign it to anyCustomer01, a variable of type ANY. To fulfill the center of Figure 4.7 we then assign anyCustomer01 to the value variable myCustomer02.

```
Record MyCustomerType type BasicRecord
    ID INT;
    name STRING;
end

Program myProgram type BasicProgram

    Function main()
        myCustomer01, myCustomer02 MyCustomerType;
        myCustomer01.ID = 130;
        myCustomer01.name = "MC Press";

        anyCustomer01 ANY = myCustomer01;
        myCustomer02 = anyCustomer01;

        sysLib.writeStdOut(anyCustomer01.ID);      // 130
        sysLib.writeStdOut(anyCustomer01.name);    // MC Press
        sysLib.writeStdOut(myCustomer02.ID);       // 130
        sysLib.writeStdOut(myCustomer02.name);     // MC Press
    end
end
```

Listing 4.4: Assigning a Reference Variable to a Value Variable

Assigning a Record that Includes a Reference Field

In earlier examples, we worked with a record that contained fields of the value types INT and STRING. The record was based on **MyCustomerType**, which is defined here.

```
Record MyCustomerType type BasicRecord
    ID INT;
    name STRING;
end
```

We now add a field that is of a reference type, and the additional field has no effect on the assignment relationships that we described earlier. However, the runtime behavior may seem different because the new field references a data area instead of containing a data area. We'll review the issue with a single example that uses the following updated version of **MyCustomerType**.

```
Record MyCustomerType type BasicRecord
    ID INT;
    name STRING;
    contact STRING[]{};
end
```

Our example copies a basic record to a variable of type ANY, as originally illustrated in Figure 4.4. Figure 4.8 includes the new **contact** field.

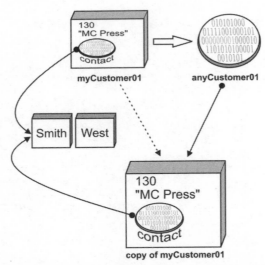

Figure 4.8: *Assigning a Value Variable to a Reference Variable, with a Difference*

Here's the updated code.

```
Record MyCustomerType type BasicRecord
    ID INT;
    name STRING;
    contact STRING[]{};
end
Program myProgram type BasicProgram
    Function main()
        myCustomer01 MyCustomerType;
        myCustomer01.ID = 130;
        myCustomer01.name = "MC Press";
        myCustomer01.contact.appendElement("Smith");
        myCustomer01.contact.appendElement("West");

        anyCustomer01 ANY = myCustomer01;
        anyCustomer01.name = "IBM";
        anyCustomer01.contact[1] = "Jones";

        sysLib.writeStdOut(myCustomer01.ID);         // 130
        sysLib.writeStdOut(myCustomer01.name);       // MC Press
        sysLib.writeStdOut(myCustomer01.contact[1]); // Jones
        sysLib.writeStdOut(anyCustomer01.ID);        // 130
        sysLib.writeStdOut(anyCustomer01.name);      // IBM
        sysLib.writeStdOut(anyCustomer01.contact[1]);// Jones
    end
end
```

Listing 4.5: Assigning a Record that Holds a Reference Variable

In two cases, the function **appendElement** adds an element of type STRING to the array referenced by **contact**. As in our earlier example, the assignment of **myCustomer01** to **anyCustomer01** copies the content of **myCustomer01** to a separate data area and causes **anyCustomer01** to refer to that area. The difference now is that both **myCustomer01** and **anyCustomer01** refer to a data area that itself references a data area.

The assignment of *IBM* to **anyCustomer01.name** still does not affect the value of **myCustomer01.name**. However, the assignment of *Jones* to **anyCustomer01.contact[1]** changes the value of **myCustomer01.contact[1]**.

Adding a Record to an Array of Records

Now that we've assigned a record that references a dynamic array, we'll consider the same issue with a slight twist: adding a record to an array of records. The next example considers the array-specific function

appendElement and is similar to the previous example for the following reason: **appendElement** adds a copy of data to an array, leaving the original data unaffected. Figure 4.9 shows the effect of the next example, illustrating the **appendElement** invocation with a dark arrow.

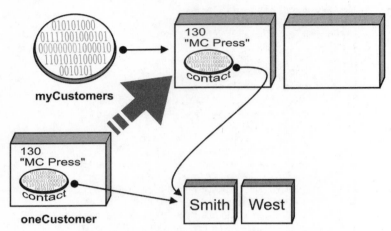

Figure 4.9: Appending a Record to a Dynamic Array

The example program uses the following Record parts.

```
Record MyCustomerType type BasicRecord
    ID INT;
    name STRING;
    contact MyContactType[]{};
end

Record MyContactType type BasicRecord
    lastName STRING;
end
```

The program builds a record named **oneCustomer** and appends it to **myCustomers**, which is an array of records.

```
Program myProgram type BasicProgram
   Function main()
      myCustomers MyCustomerType[]{};
      oneCustomer MyCustomerType;
      oneContact  MyContactType;

      // build oneCustomer
      oneCustomer.ID = 130;
      oneCustomer.name = "MC Press";
      oneContact.lastName = "Smith";
      oneCustomer.contact.appendElement(oneContact);
      oneContact.lastName = "West";
      oneCustomer.contact.appendElement(oneContact);

      // append oneCustomer and then change it
      myCustomers.appendElement(oneCustomer);
      oneCustomer.contact[1].lastName = "Jones";

      // is the update to myCustomers intended?
      sysLib.writeStdOut
         (myCustomers[1].contact[1].lastName);      // Jones
   end
end
```

Listing 4.6: Adding a Record that Contains Reference Variables

The data area to which the **oneCustomer.contact** refers contains the contact list; and that area is identical to the area to which **myCustomers[1].contact** refers. Even after you append **oneCustomer**, some changes that you might have thought would affect only **oneCustomer** also affect **myCustomers**. If you are working with **appendElement** or **insertElement**, you need to be aware of this behavior.

Expressions

An *expression* is a sequence of operands such as constants, variables, literals, and function invocations; operators such as + and -, and special characters such as parentheses. At run time, each expression resolves to a value of a specific type:

- A *numeric expression* resolves to a number of a specific type. The language supports modulus and exponentiation and offers system functions for trigonometry, logarithms, rounding, and numeric comparisons.

- A *text expression* resolves to a value of a character-based type such as STRING or UNICODE. The language supports concatenation and substring processing.

- A *logical expression* resolves to *true* or *false*. Its purpose is to affect the flow of logic in the EGL statements **case** and **if**, which run conditionally, and in statements such as **for** and **while**, which run iteratively.

  To compare two numeric, text, or datetime expressions, you can use the following operators: equality (==), inequality (!=), and the variations of less-than or greater-than (<, >, <=, >=). You can test a variable's content; for example, is it numeric? is it blank? does it conform to a particular string pattern? You can test for the target system in which the code is running; for example, is the code running on AIX? You can determine whether a particular value is in a data table or array by using the **in** operator. You can use the *not* (!) operator to reverse the value of a logical expression; for example, from *true* to *false*. Last, you can combine logical expressions with the *and* (**&&**) or *or* (||) operator.

- A *date/time expression* resolves to a date, interval, time, or time-stamp. You can subtract a timestamp from a timestamp to find the interval between the two values, for example, and can add two intervals to calculate a third. A variety of functions are available, too; for example, to return a date value from a timestamp.

Expressions are evaluated in accordance with a set of precedence rules and, within a given level of precedence, from left to right. However, you can use parentheses to force a different ordering.

Name Resolution in Expressions

Earlier, we described rules for resolving type and part names. Those rules are meaningful primarily in relation to data declarations. A second set of rules is meaningful primarily in the EGL logic statements, for resolving identifiers in expressions.

The main rules of this second kind are similar to those in other languages. Given an expression such as **myVar01 + myVar02**, for example, EGL first considers *local names*, which are identifiers declared within the function where the expression resides. Included in this category are the names of function parameters and of function-specific variables and constants.

If a name in the expression is not matched by a local name, EGL searches in the next category of names, and then (if the name is still unresolved) searches in the next. Eight categories of names are in effect; but in many cases you'll need to be aware only of local names and three other categories, in the following order:

- Program-global names, which identify variables, parameters, and constants that are global to the program or handler in which the function resides

- Run-unit global names, which identify variables and constants that reside in libraries and are available to all logic in the run unit.

- The names of EGL system variables.

You can avoid problems in name resolution if you use container names as qualifiers. If the field **employeeNumber** is in a record named **employee**, for example, you can—and, in some cases, must—use the following syntax.

```
employee.employeeNumber
```

You can use library names as qualifiers and can use package names, as may be necessary when referencing variables and constants that are in libraries, forms, or data tables.

To access an identifier that is program-global even when a local identifier takes precedence, qualify the identifier with the keyword **this**, as in the following example.

```
Program myProgram

   category INT;

   function main()
      category INT;

      // this.category refers to the program-global variable
      this.category = 4;
   end
end
```

Assignment and Reference Compatibility

Compatibility rules tell when an expression of a given type is valid during an exchange of data in memory. The rules apply to an assignment statement, or when a function return value is received into a variable, or when an argument is passed to a function. Two sets of rules apply:

- *Assignment compatibility* is in effect in most cases; for example, when your code assigns an expression of a CHAR type to a STRING type or to some other value variable.

- *Reference compatiblity* is in effect in other cases; for example, when you are assigning, passing, or returning a reference variable to a reference variable.

Details are in the Rational Business Developer help system.

Static and Dynamic Access

In most cases, your code interacts with a variable statically, which means that at generation time, all the details necessary to ensure variable access are in place. Each reference to the variable is built with a dot syntax such as **employee.employeeAddress.city**, as shown in the following example.

```
Record AddressPart
   streeAddress STRING;
   city STRING;
   state STRING;
end

Record EmployeePart
   employeeNumber  SMALLINT;
   employeeAddress AddressPart;
end

Program myProgram

   Function main()
      employee EmployeePart;
      employee.employeeAddress.city = "San Diego";
   end
end
```

The variable name is known to the code at generation time but is not retained at run time because by then, the name has been replaced by a known (static) memory address.

Static access is fast because the EGL runtime does not need to locate the variable or to verify that the access is valid for the data type. The drawback of static access is a lack of flexibility; but for many business uses, the flexibility is unimportant.

In contrast to the variable in the previous example, a variable of type ANY is accessed dynamically, which means that the EGL runtime locates the variable by name and ensures that the access is valid. Dynamic access occurs, for example, if your logic assigns any of several types of records to a variable of type ANY and then accesses a record field. In the following code, a variable called **person** is accessed dynamically, with each successive field identified by a bracketed string.

```
Record AddressPart
   streetAddress STRING;
   city STRING;
end

Record EmployeePart
   employeeNumber  SMALLINT;
   employeeAddress AddressPart;
end

Record RetireePart
   employeeDetail EmployeePart;
   pensionType CHAR(1);
end

Program myProgram

   Function main()

      isRetiree Boolean = false;
      employee EmployeePart;
      retiree  RetireePart;
      person ANY;

      // assume other processing
      // that assigns values to isRetiree
      // as well as to person, which receives
      // a record of type employee or
      // a record of type retiree
      if (isRetiree)
         person["employeeDetail"]["employeeAddress"]["city"]
            = "San Diego";
      else
         person["employeeAddress"]["city"]
            = "San Diego";
      end
   end
end
```

Listing 4.7: Dynamic Access

The bracket syntax indicates that dynamic access is in effect. The previous example showed literal strings, but a major benefit of dynamic access is that you can use variables of a character type, as in the following variation.

```
Function main()

   isRetiree Boolean = false;
   employee EmployeePart;
   retiree  RetireePart;
   fieldName01 STRING = "employeeAddress";
   fieldName02 STRING = "city";
   person ANY;

   if (!isRetiree) // if isRetiree is false
     person[fieldName01][fieldName02] = "San Diego";
   end
end
```

In most cases, the bracket syntax is optional if you have access to the literal string, so the reference just described can be **person.employeeAddress.city**. However, you must use bracket syntax when accessing an EGL dictionary entry whose key has a space or otherwise does not conform to an EGL naming convention. Consider the following code.

```
Function main()

    miscellaneous Dictionary { };
    category, component, test STRING;

    miscellaneous["Function"] = "EGL reserved word";
    miscellaneous["EGL runtime"] = "Flexible!";
    miscellaneous.dot = "You can use dot syntax here";

    category = miscellaneous["Function"];
    component = miscellaneous["EGL runtime"];
    test = miscellaneous.dot;

end
```

That code assigns "EGL reserved word" to **category**, "Flexible!" to **component**, and "You can use dot syntax here" to **test**.

CHAPTER 5

EGL System Resources

This chapter reviews three EGL resources that are available when you write functions: statements, system libraries, and a mechanism for exception handling.

Our focus remains on core EGL functionality. The help system for Rational Business Developer provides details on other areas, including the extensive EGL support for the data-access technologies DL/I and WebSphere MQ; for the transaction managers CICS and IMS; and for the user-interface technologies described as Text UI, Console UI, and Web transactions.

EGL Statements

In this section, we describe EGL statements for general use. In the next chapter, we lists statements that access files and relational databases.

Table 5-1 list the statements covered here.

Table 5-1: Selected EGL Statements for General Use	
Statement Type	Purpose
assignment	To assign the value of an expression to a data area
call	To transfer control to another program
case	To run one of several alternative sets of statements

Statement Type	Purpose
	Table 5-1: Selected EGL Statements for General Use (Continued)
comment	To document code
function invocation	To run a function
continue	To return control to the start of an enclosing loop in the same function
exit	To end the processing of the nearest enclosing statement of a stated kind
for	To define a block of statements that run in a loop until a specified value is reached
forward	To transfer control from a JSF handler to (in most cases) a Web page
if, else	To define a block of statements that run if and only if a specified condition applies; also, to define an alternative block
move	To copy data from a source to a target, with processing not available in assignment statements
return	To return control from a function and optionally to return a value to the invoker
set	To establish characteristics of a record or record field.
transfer	To transfer control from one main program to another
while	To define a block of statements that run in a loop until a test fails

Code Documentation

A comment lets you add documentation to your code and is useful almost anywhere in an EGL source file, not only in functions.

A single-line comment begins with double slashes (//), as shown next, in boldface.

```
i INT = 2;

// a while loop follows
while(i > 0)
    sysLib.writeStdOut(i);
    i = i-1
end
```

A comment that can span multiple lines begins with a slash and asterisk (/*) and ends with an asterisk and slash (*/), as shown next.

```
i INT = 2;

/* a while loop
    does not follow */
sysLib.writeStdOut(i);
```

Data Assignment

You assign data by coding the assignment, **move**, and **set** statements.

Assignment

The primary data-assignment statement copies an expression into a data area. In the following example, **fullString** receives the value *Welcome to EGL*.

```
oneString, fullString STRING;
oneString = "Welcome ";
fullString = oneString + "to EGL";
```

Move

The **move** statement copies data from a source area to a target area, in any of three ways. First, byte by byte; second, by matching the field names in the target and source; and third, by matching the field positions in the target and source. The **move** statement provides additional options for copying values from one array to another.

Here are two Record parts.

```
Record MyCustomerOneType type BasicRecord
    ID INT;
    title STRING;
end

Record MyCustomerTwoType type BasicRecord
    age INT;
    title STRING;
end
```

Here are two declarations.

```
myCustomer01 MyCustomerOneType;
myCustomer02 MyCustomerTwoType;
```

The effect of **move** by name is to copy the values only for fields whose names match. The result of the next example is to copy a value from one field named **title** to another.

```
myCustomer01.ID = 25;
myCustomer01.title = "Doctor";
myCustomer02.age = 40;
myCustomer02.title = "Officer";
move myCustomer01 to myCustomer02 byname;

sysLib.writeStdOut(myCustomer02.age);   // 40
sysLib.writeStdOut(myCustomer02.name);  // Doctor
```

In contrast, the effect of **move** by position is to copy the values for each field in a record, without regard to the field names. .

```
myCustomer01.ID = 25;
myCustomer01.title = "Doctor";
myCustomer02.age = 40;
myCustomer02.title = "Officer";
move myCustomer01 to myCustomer02 byposition;

sysLib.writeStdOut(myCustomer02.age);   // 25
sysLib.writeStdOut(myCustomer02.name);  // Doctor
```

The last example is with arrays. The assumption in each of the following cases is that the target array has the number of elements needed to accept the content being copied.

```
// move "Buy" to elements 2, 3, and 4 in temp
move "Buy" to temp[2] for 3;

// move elements 2, 4, and 4 from temp
//      into elements 5, 6, and 7 in final
move temp[2] to final[5] for 3;
```

Set

The **set** statement establishes characteristics of a record, form, or field. The statement has many variations. For example, in relation to a record, you can reset the field values to those initially specified in the Record part definition. The boldface statement in the following code has that effect.

```
Record DepartmentPart type BasicRecord
   Department STRING = "Sales";
   BudgetCode INT;
end
Function MyFunction()
   MyDept DepartmentPart;
   SysLib.writeStdOut(MyDept.Department);
   MyDept.Department = "Marketing";
   SysLib.writeStdOut(MyDept.Department);
   set MyDept.Department initial;
   SysLib.writeStdOut(MyDept.Department);
end
```

The code writes **Sales** and then **Marketing** and then **Sales**.

Conditional Processing

The **if** and embedded **else** statements provide conditional processing, as does the **case** statement.

If, Else

The **if** statement defines a block of statements that run if and only if a specified condition applies. The **else** statement defines an alternative block of statements.

The following code sets msgText in various cases. If msgStatus equals 1, msgText is set to *Yes!*; if msgStatus equals 0, msgText is set to *No!*; and otherwise, msgText is set to *Service invocation failed.*

```
if (msgStatus == 1)
    msgText = "Yes!";
else
    if (msgStatus == 0)
        msgText = "No!";
    else
        msgText = "Service invocation failed!";
    end
end
```

Case

The **case** statement runs one of several alternative sets of statements.

You can specify a value for comparison, as shown next.

```
case (msgStatus)
    when(1)
        msgText = "Yes!";
    when(0)
        mgText = "No!";
    otherwise
        msgText = "Service invocation failed!";
    end
```

In this example, if **msgStatus** evaluates to 1, **msgText** receives the value *Yes!*; if **msgStatus** evaluates to 0, **msgText** receives *No!*; and if **msgStatus** evaluates to any other value, **msgText** receives *Service invocation failed!*

The **case** statement runs all statements in a given **when** or **otherwise** clause, and control never passes to more than one clause. In the next example, if

myCode evaluates to 1, the functions **myFunction01** and **myFunction02** run and the others do not.

```
case (myCode)
  when (1)
     myFunction01();
     myFunction02();
  when (2, 3, 4)
     myFunction03();
  otherwise
     myDefaultFunction();
end
```

If you don't specify a value for comparison, the **case** statement runs the first clause for which a condition resolves to *true*. In the following example, if **myCode** evaluates to 4, the function **myFunction03** runs.

```
case
  when (myCode == 3)
     myFunction01();
  when (myCode > 3)
     myFunction03();
  otherwise
     myDefaultFunction();
end
```

Loop Control

The **for, while,** and **continue** statements provide loop control.

For

The **for** statement defines a block of statements that run in a loop until a specified value is exceeded. For example, the following code writes the numbers 10, 20, 30, and 40 to the standard output.

```
for (i int from 10 to 40 by 10)
   sysLib.writeStdOut(i);
end
```

The following code writes the numbers 40, 30, 20, and 10.

```
for (i int from 40 to 10 decrement by 10)
    sysLib.writeStdOut(i);
end
```

While

The **while** statement defines a block of statements that run in a loop until a test fails. The following code writes the numbers 10, 20, 30, and 40.

```
i INT = 10;
while (i <= 40)
    sysLib.writeStdOut(i);
    i = i + 10;
end
```

Continue

The **continue** statement returns control to the start of an enclosing loop in the same function. For example, the following code writes the numbers 1, 2, and 4 to the standard output.

```
for (i int from 1 to 4 by 1)
    if (i == 3)
        continue;
    end
    sysLib.writeStdOut(i);
end
```

Transfer of Control Within a Program

Function invocations and the **return** and **exit** statements transfer control within a program or handler.

Function Invocation

A function invocation runs a function and includes arguments to match the function parameters. The arguments must match the parameters in number, with some variation allowed in the data type, as specified in compatibility rules.

The next statement passes a string to a function.

```
myFunction("test this string");
```

If a function returns a value, two rules apply. First, you can code a variable to receive that value from the function, but the variable is not required. Second, you can code the function invocation inside a larger expression. For example, if the function in the next expression returns the name *Smith*, the string sent to the standard output is *Customer 23 is Smith*.

```
sysLib.writeStdOut("Customer 23 is "
                    + getCustomerName(23));
```

Return

The **return** statement returns control from a function and optionally returns a value to the invoker. In the next example, the statement returns 0.

```
for (i int from 10 to 40 by 10)
   sysLib.writeStdOut(i);
end
return(0);
```

Exit

The **exit** statement ends the processing of the nearest enclosing statement of a stated kind. For example, the following code stops processing the **for** statement when the value if i is 3.

```
for (i int from 1 to 4 by 1)
  if (i == 3)
    exit for;
  end
  sysLib.writeStdOut(i);
end
```

The code writes the numbers 1 and 2 to the standard output.

Transfer of Control Out of a Program

The **call**, **forward**, and **transfer** statements transfer control to logic that's outside the program or handler.

Call

The **call** statement transfers control to another program. The arguments must match the program parameters in number and type.

```
myCustomerNumber = 23;
myCustomerName = "Smith";
call myProgram(myCustomerNumber, myCustomerName);
```

Forward

The **forward** statement in a JSF handler transfers control; in most cases, to another Web page.

```
forward to "myWebPage";
```

The current example forwards control to the logic that the JavaServer Faces runtime identifies as *myWebPage*. In most cases, that logic is (essentially) a Web page. We cover JavaServer Faces in later chapters.

Transfer

The **transfer** statement transfers control from one main program to another, ending the first program and optionally passing a record. The following code transfers control to **Program02** and passes a record named **myRecord**.

```
transfer to Program Program02 passing myRecord;
```

System Libraries

In addition to developing libraries that include variables, constants, and functions, you can access EGL system libraries such as the following ones.

- The **sysLib** library lets you write to an error log or a standard location, commit or roll back database changes, retrieve properties and messages from text files, wait for time to elapse, or run an operating-system command.

- The **strLib** library lets you format date and time variables and manipulate strings.

- The **mathLib** library lets you perform common mathematical and trigonometric operations. You can round a number in various ways and determine the maximum or minimum of two numbers.

- The **datetimeLib** library lets you retrieve the current date and time and lets you process dates, times, and intervals in various ways.

- The **serviceLib** library lets you specify a service location to be accessed at run time.

- The **lobLib** library lets EGL-generated Java code work with variables of type BLOB (binary large object) or CLOB (character large object). You can associate a file with a variable of one of those types, transfer data to and from the file, and gain access to a string that represents the data.

Some libraries are specific to a runtime technology; for example:

- The **sqlLib** library lets you interact with relational database management systems; for example, to connect to a database at run time.

- The **j2eeLib** library lets you interact with a Web application server from an EGL JSF handler.

Exception Handling

EGL-generated code can encounter an exception during the following runtime operations: a program call or transfer; access of a service or library; a function invocation; access of persistent storage; a data comparison; or a data assignment. You also can *throw*—register—an exception in response to some runtime event; for example, a user's entering an invalid customer ID at a Web browser.

To make an exception available to be *caught*—that is, to be handled—you embed business logic inside a **try** block. Here's an outline of a **try** block.

```
try
    // place your business logic here

    onException
        (exceptionRecord ExceptionType01)
        // handle the exception here

    onException
        (exceptionRecord ExceptionType02)
        // handle the exception here
end
```

The **try** block includes zero to many **onException** blocks. Each **onException** block is essentially an error handler and is similar to a function that accepts a single parameter—an exception record—and returns no value. Unlike a function, the **onException** block has no **end** statement; instead, the block ends at the start of the next **onException** block, if any, or at the bottom of the **try** block.

The use of a **try** block has a performance cost, so you may decide to embed only the most exception-prone code in such a block.

In the following example, the attempt to add content to an uninitialized array causes an exception that we describe with the phrase "**NullValueException.**"

```
Program myProgram type BasicProgram
    myStringArray STRING[];
    Function main()
        try
            myStringArray.appendElement("One"); // error
            onException (exception NullValueException)
                myStringArray = new STRING[];
                sysLib.writeStdErr ("NullValueException");
            onException (exception AnyException)
                sysLib.writeStdErr ("AnyException");
        end

        sysLib.writeStdErr
            ("Size of array is " +
                myStringArray.getSize());
    end
end
```

In this example, an **onException** block catches the exception, initializes the array, and writes the name of the exception type to the standard error output. A statement outside the **try** block then writes the following string to that output: *Size of array is 0.*

In general, the exception is caught by the first **onException** block that is specific to the exception type; here, the type is NullValueException. However, if no onException block is specific to the exception type, the EGL runtime invokes the **AnyException** block, if any. The placement of the **AnyException** block in the list of **OnException** blocks is not meaningful; the **AnyException** block is invoked only as a last resort.

An **OnException** block can itself include try blocks, to any level of nesting. In the following example, a statement in a **try** block also throws a **NullValueException**.

```
Program myProgram type BasicProgram
   myStringArray STRING[];
   myStringArray02 STRING[];
   Function main()
      try
         myStringArray.appendElement("One");
         onException (e01 NullValueException)
            try
               myStringArray.appendElement("One");
               onException
                  (e02 NullValueException)
                  myStringArray = new STRING[];
                  myStringArray.appendElement("One");
            end
      end
      sysLib.writeStdErr
         ("Size of array is " +
         myStringArray.getSize());
   end
end
```

The last statement in the example writes the string *Size of array is 1.*

We say that an exception is *cleared* if the code continues running without being interrupted again by that exception. The exception is cleared in the following two cases: the exception causes invocation of an **OnException** block at the current nesting level; or the exception occurs in a **try** block that has no **OnException** handlers at all. That second case has little practical value because you probably don't want your code to continue running unless you first correct the error or at least log the details.

The function ends immediately in the following case: an exception occurs and the **try** block at the current nesting level includes **onException** blocks, but none of the blocks catches the exception.

Propagation

The next example of error handling is similar to an earlier one, but the business logic in this case invokes the function **appendToArray**, which in turn invokes the function **doAppend**.

```
Program myProgram type BasicProgram
   myStringArray STRING[];
   Function main()
      try
         appendToArray("One");
         onException (exception NullValueException)
            myStringArray = new STRING[];
            sysLib.writeStdErr ("NullValueException");
      end

      sysLib.writeStdErr
         ("Size of array is " +
            myStringArray.getSize());
   end
   Function appendToArray (theInput STRING IN)
      doAppend(theInput);
      sysLib.writeStdErr ("You won't see the message." );
   end
   Function doAppend (theString STRING IN)
      myStringArray.appendElement(theString);
      sysLib.writeStdErr ("You won't see the message." );
   end
end
```

Listing 5.1: Propagation of exception

The **NullValueException** exception now occurs in **doAppend**, but the exception is handled as before, in the **main** function.

Figure 5.1 illustrates the general rule.

If a function throws an error that is not cleared, the function immediately ends, and the exception *propagates*—moves its influence—to the function's invoker, which clears the error or immediately ends. An uncleared exception propagates to the immediate invoker and then to progressively higher-level invokers until the exception is cleared or the program ends.

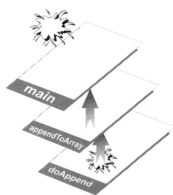

An exception also propagates from a called program to progressively higher-level callers. However, a failed service returns ServiceInvocationException, regardless of the exception that caused the service failure.

Figure 5.1: Propagation

Exception Fields

Two fields—**message** and **messageID**—are available in every exception record. In relation to an exception that is defined by EGL, the **message** field contains a series of messages, each with an error number, and the **messageID** field contains the error numbers alone. For example, we might have coded one of our earlier **OnException** blocks as follows.

```
onException (exception NullValueException)
   myStringArray = new STRING[];
   sysLib.writeStdErr
      ("Handled this issue: \n" + exception.message);
```

In EGL-generated Java code, the new-line character (**\n**) makes the first error message appear on a new line, as shown next.

```
Handled this issue:
EGL0098E The reference variable named myStringArray is null.
EGL0002I The error occurred in the myProgram program.
```

Our next example shows a way to throw an exception of your own. We begin with an SQL Record part and an Exception part.

```
Record MyCustomerRecord type SQLRecord
    { keyItems = [customerNumber],
      tableNames = [["Customer"]] }
    customerNumber STRING;
    creditScore INT;
end

Record CustomerException type Exception
    customerID STRING;
end
```

After we declare a record that is based on the SQL Record part, we assign a customer number and code an EGL **get** statement to retrieve details about the customer identified by that number. The logic is similar to what is shown here.

```
myCustomer MyCustomerRecord;
myCustomer.customerNumber = "A1234";
get myCustomer;
```

We ignore the need to handle an SQL exception but show how to throw an exception of your own. In the following program, the CustomerException block uses the following fields: **customerID**, which was defined explicitly in the CustomerException part, and **message**, which is of type STRING and is present in any Exception record.

```
Program myProgram type BasicProgram

    Function main()
        myCustomer MyCustomerRecord;
        myCustomer.customerNumber = "A1234";
        try
            retrieveOne(myCustomer);
            onException (exception CustomerException)
                sysLib.writeStdErr
                    ("Customer: " + exception.customerID
                    + "\nIssue: " + exception.message);
        end
    end
```

Listing 5.2: Throwing an Exception (part 1)

```
Function retrieveOne(theCustomer MyCustomerRecord)
    get theCustomer;
    if (theCustomer.creditScore < 310)
        throw new CustomerException
            { customerID = theCustomer.customerNumber,
              message = "No Credit" };
    end
  end
end
```

Listing 5.2: Throwing an Exception (part 2)

After the get statement runs, the record **theCustomer** includes the credit score for the customer whose number is A1234. If the score is less than 310, the **throw** statement creates a new record, initializing the record fields for use in the **CustomerException** block. The output is as follows.

```
Customer: A1234
Issue: No Credit
```

CHAPTER 6

Files and Relational Databases

E GL lets you access files and message queues without requiring that you know details of the access technologies. A further convenience is that you can use the same EGL file-access statements to interact with databases.

In this chapter, we list the data-access statements and give examples of their use with serial files and relational databases. We begin by describing how EGL handles an issue that affects most applications.

Logical Unit of Work

A *logical unit of work* is a set of changes to persistent storage, such that all the changes are *committed*—made permanent—or *rolled back*—revoked—as if they were a single change. For example, the transfer of money between two bank accounts is a two-stage process that subtracts a value from one account and adds a value to another. The two changes are a logical unit of work because they must occur together or not at all.

A logical unit of work applies to some kinds of persistent storage and not to others. For example, your code can roll back its changes to a relational database by invoking a single function, sysLib.rollback; but that function has no effect on a Windows-platform serial file. Your code can only compensate for an earlier change to such a file, perhaps by making a second change to the same file or by adding an entry to an error log. We say that the relational database is *recoverable* and that the serial file is *non-recoverable*.

A logical unit of work begins when your code changes a recoverable resource and ends at the point of commit or rollback. A commit occurs if your code runs sysLib.commit or if the EGL runtime causes an implicit commit; as occurs, for example, when the first program in a run unit ends successfully. A rollback occurs if your code runs sysLib.rollback or if the EGL runtime causes an implicit rollback; as occurs, for example, after an uncaught exception.

Several resources can be recoverable, including databases, VSAM files on CICS, and WebSphere MQ message queues. In your EGL code, a logical unit of work applies to all the recoverable resources that your code changes.

Data-Access Statements

Table 6-1 lists the major EGL data-access statements for files and relational databases.

Table 6-1: Kinds of EGL Data-Access Statements	
Statement Type	**Purpose**
add	To place a record in a file, message queue, or database; or to place a set of records in a database.
close	To close the file or message queue associated with a given record; to disconnect from a printer; or, in the case of an SQL record, to close the *cursor*—a list of database rows—that was made available by an EGL open or get statement.
delete	To remove a record from a file, or a row from a relational database.
execute	To run one or more SQL statements; in particular, SQL data-definition statements such as CREATE TABLE; and data-manipulation statements such as INSERT or UPDATE.
get	To retrieve a single file record or database row or to retrieve a set of database rows. The retrieval may allow for a subsequent update or delete.
forEach	To process data from each of several database rows returned from an open or get statement.
open	To select a set of rows from a relational database.
prepare	To specify an SQL PREPARE statement, which builds a database-access statement at run time
replace	To put a changed record into a file or database.

File Access

An EGL Record part can be the basis of a variable used as the source or target of an I/O operation. For example, here's a Record part used as the basis of a serial record.

```
Record MyRecordPart type SerialRecord
   { FileName="Inner" }
   PolicyID CHAR(15);
end
```

Here's a related record declaration and assignment, followed by an EGL add statement that places data from the record into a file.

```
myRecord MyRecordPart;
myRecord.PolicyID = "A1234";
try
   add myRecord;
   onException(except FileIOException)
      ;
end
```

In this case, the record myRecord is said to be the *I/O object* of the add statement.

We can retrieve data back into the same record by closing the file and writing a get statement. Here's the code.

```
try
   close myRecord;
   myRecord.PolicyID = "";
   get next myRecord;
   onException(except FileIOException)
      ;
end
sysLib.writeStdOut(myRecord.PolicyID);
```

Despite our having cleared the PolicyID field in the second line, the last line in the example displays the value *A1234*, which was retrieved from the same file as the one that received the data. But what file was acccessed?

File Names and Resource Associations

The only file name previously in our example is the setting of the FileName annotation, in the Record part MyRecordPart.

```
Record MyRecordPart type SerialRecord
    { FileName="Inner" }
    PolicyID CHAR(15);
end
```

The FileName setting is known as the *logical file name* and does not specify the name of a *physical file*, which is a storage location on the target platform.

Resource Associations Part

Before you generate EGL code, you configure a *build descriptor*, which is a build part that guides the generation process and references other definitions. If a record in your logic accesses a physical file, you are likely to reference a *resource associations part* in the build descriptor. The resource associations part can associate the logical file name with a physical file on each target platform where you intend to run your code.

In essence, the resource associations part provides a table like the one shown next, where the phrase *system name* refers to the physical file's system-specific name,

file name	system type	system name
Inner	win	c:\Outer.txt
	zosbatch	MYFILE

The table indicates that the logical file name *Inner* is associated with one file if the code runs on a Microsoft Windows platform, and another file if the code runs as a z/OS batch program.

The benefit of this mechanism is that, at generation time, a change to the resource associations part redirects runtime processing to a different file. In this way, you can change from a test environment to a production environment without changing your code.

In our resource associations part, the system name specified for z/OS batch was itself a logical file name. The implication is that on z/OS, a switch from one physical file to another is possible at deployment time.

ResourceAssociation Field

You can determine, in your code, what physical file was accessed by retrieving the value of the field resourceAssociation. That field is present in every Record part whose stereotype is primarily for file I/O, as is the case for a SerialRecord part. Here's how we retrieve the file name from a record that's based on MyRecordPart.

```
sysLib.writeStdOut(myRecord.resourceAssociation);
```

We'll hereafter assuming that the code is running on a Microsoft Windows platform, where the file name is "c:\Outer.txt".

You can also redirect processing in your code—for example, in response to user input—by setting the field resourceAssociation, as shown next.

```
myRecord.resourceAssociation = "c:\\Outer02.txt";
myRecord.policyID = "Z4321";
try
   add myRecord;
   onException(exceptRecord FileIOException)
      ;
end
```

The assignment of a physical file name to resourceAssociation writes *Z4321* to the file c:\Outer02.txt.

Escape Character

We'll digress briefly to clarify a point of syntax. In that last example, the two backslashes in the file name are needed because the first is the EGL *escape character*, which is not processed as other characters are processed.

An escape character allows use of a subsequent character in a context where the subsequent character would interfere with the desired behavior. For example, a quote mark within a string would end the string prematurely. You avoid that outcome by preceding the quote mark with an escape character, as in the following example.

```
quote STRING = "You might say, \"Forget about it!\"";
```

Support for Relational Databases

The basic idea of a relational database is that data is stored in persistent tables. Each table column represents a discrete unit of data such as an order ID or an order-status code, and each row represents a collection of such data. In short, a table row is equivalent to a file record.

In most cases, one or more columns in a database table are *primary keys*, which means that the values in those columns are unique to a given row. If multiple columns are primary keys, the sequence of column values must be unique to a given row.

Access to relational databases is by way of Structured Query Language (SQL). For some interactions, you don't need to know SQL at all. However, many enterprise applications use complex database queries, requiring that you have expertise with the language or that someone on your development project has such expertise.

You can interact with a relational database as follows: define a Record part whose stereotype is SQLRecord, create a variable based on that Record part, and use the variable as an I/O object in different data-access statements.

Insertion and Retrieval

Here's an example Record part.

```
Record OrderPart type sqlRecord {
      tablenames=[["ORDERS"]],
      keyItems=[orderID] }

   orderID INT
      { Column="ID" };
   orderStatus CHAR(1)
      { Column="STATUS" };
end
```

Each field in the Record part is associated with a table column, as indicated by use of the Column annotation. By associating a record field and a column, you ensure that when an SQL record is used in a data-access statement at run time, data passes from field to column or from column to field. If a Record-part field name is the same as the corresponding table-column name, you don't need to set the Column annotation.

The Record part as a whole has two annotation fields. First, the tableNames annotation field identifies a single table, but could indicate that the part provides access to a *join*, which is conbination of tables. For example, a join of two tables might be necessary to access all the item details for a given order. Second, the keyItems annotation field lists the *key fields*, which are, in most cases, the Record part fields that correspond to the unique keys in the table. However, the key fields may refer to other columns, as can be useful to exploit the default behavior of EGL data-access statements in different ways.

Here's a record declaration and field assignments, along with an EGL add statement that places data from the record into the database table ORDERS.

```
myRecord OrderPart;
myRecord.orderID = 123;
myRecord.orderStatus = "1";
try
   add myRecord;
   onException(except SQLException)
     ;
end
```

To retrieve a row, you assign a value to the record field associated with the key column and then issue a get statement, as in the next example, which retrieves the row we just added.

```
myRecord.orderID = 123;
try
   get myRecord;
   onException(except SQLException)
     ;
end
```

Implicit and Explicit SQL Statements

For a given EGL statement, the generated code issues one or more SQL statements in accordance with details specified in the Record part. For example, in place of the the EGL add statement, the generated code issues an SQL INSERT statement, which adds one or more rows to the table. In our current example, the INSERT statement adds a single row to the table, placing a value in every column. The SQL code includes EGL variables such as myRecord.orderID.

```
insert into ORDERS
    ( ORDERS.ID,
      ORDERS.STATUS )
values
    ( :myRecord.orderID,
      :myRecord.orderStatus )
```

You don't need to understand SQL or to see the SQL code during development. The code is implicit in the EGL statement. However, you can make the SQL code explicit, as follows: right-click on the EGL statement name in Rational Business Developer, select **SQL Statement**, and click **Add** (meaning "add the SQL statement"). The EGL statement itself is now expressed differently.

```
add myRecord with
#sql{
    insert into ORDERS
        ( ORDERS.ID,
          ORDERS.STATUS )
    values
        ( :myRecord.orderID,
          :myRecord.orderStatus )};
```

When the SQL statement is explicit, you can revise it in your EGL code, but changes to the Record part have no effect on how the EGL statement interacts with the database. Explicit statements takes precedence over implicit ones.

If you make explicit the SQL statement that's related to the EGL get statement, the EGL statement is expressed as follows.

```
get myRecord with
#sql{
   select
     ORDERS.ID,
     ORDERS.STATUS
   from ORDERS
   where
      ORDERS.ID = :myRecord.orderID};
```

The WHERE clause in any SQL SELECT statement restricts what rows are retrieved. In this case, the SELECT statement retrieves only those rows for which the ID column equals the value specified in the EGL field orderID.

In general, the following rules apply to an EGL get statement for which an SQL record is the I/O object:

- The implicit SQL SELECT statement retrieves data into all the fields listed in the Record part.

- The implicit WHERE clause restricts the retrieved rows to those for which as many as two conditions apply: the value in each key field is found in the related column; and the *default select condition* is fulfilled, as shown in the next section.

Open and ForEach

The open statement gives you a way to identify a set of rows, and the forEach statement provides an elegant way to process them. We'll show one of many possible variations.

Here's the Record part we used earlier, with a revision in boldface.

```
Record OrderPart type sqlRecord {
       tablenames=[["ORDERS"]],
       keyItems=[orderID],
       defaultSelectCondition=#sqlCondition{STATUS = '2'} }

    orderID INT
       { Column="ID" };
    orderStatus CHAR(1)
       { Column="STATUS" };
end
```

In our use of the open statement, the implicit SQL statement selects only the table rows that fulfill two requirements:

- The value in the ID column is greater than or equal to the value in the orderID field. The value of the annotation field keyItems sets this requirement.

- The STATUS column is equal to 2. The value of the annotation field defaultSelectCondition sets this requirement.

In this case, the annotation field keyItems also ensures that the rows are returned in ascending ID order. The field has no affect on ordering if keyItems refers to multiple key fields.

Here's the code.

```
oneOrder OrderPart;
oneOrder.ID = 400
try
    open myResultSet for oneOrder;

    forEach (oneOrder)
       sysLib.writeStdOut
          (oneOrder.orderStatus + " " +
             oneOrder.orderID);
    end

    onException (except SQLException)
       ;
end
```

The open statement identifies a name for the set of rows returned by the statement. That name—here, *myResultSet*—lets you associate the open statement with another EGL statement that acts on the result set. The name is not used in the current example, though. Instead, the forEach statement accesses each retrieved row in turn and processes it, writing the following strings to the standard output.

```
2 456
2 789
```

You can specify additional details in the open statement, for the purpose of overriding the default selection and ordering behaviors.

In passing, we'll note that the open statement is often used in *dynamic SQL*, which is a mechanism for structuring the SQL statement WHERE clause at run time so that, for example, user input can determine many aspects of a database search.

Dynamic Arrays of SQL Records

You can use dynamic arrays of SQL records to add or retrieve data from a relational database. To show this, we'll rely on our previous SQL Record part, which included the annotation field defaultSelectCondition.

First, we declare an array of records and add three rows to an otherwise empty database table.

```
myOrder OrderPart[3]{};
myOrder[1].orderID = 123;
myOrder[1].orderStatus = "1";
myOrder[2].orderID = 456;
myOrder[2].orderStatus = "2";
myOrder[3].orderID = 789;
myOrder[3].orderStatus = "2";

try
    add myOrder;
    onException (except SQLException)
        ;
end
```

As shown, the additions are fulfilled by coding a single EGL add statement.

Next, we'll use a get statement to retrieve the added rows into a dynamic array.

```
yourOrder myOrderPart[]{};
try
    get yourOrder;
    onException (except SQLException)
        ;
end

arraySize int = yourOrder.getSize();

for (i int from 1 to arraySize by 1)
    sysLib.writeStdOut
        (yourOrder[i].orderStatus + " " +
         yourOrder[i].orderID);
end
```

The annotation field defaultSelectCondition causes retrieval of data only from the rows for which the STATUS column value is 2. In this case, the annotation field keyItems causes retrieval of the data in ascending ID order.

The output of the logic is as follows.

```
2 456
2 789
```

Exception Handling

One of the benefits of using an EGL record for data access is that you can use the is or not operator to test the record for an error value, as in the following examples.

```
// not end of file
if (yourRecord not endOfFile)
   ;
end

// no record found
if (myRecord is noRecordFound)
   ;
end

// wrongly tried to add an existing
//    file record or database row
if (myRecord is unique)
   ;
end
```

Where in your code do such entries belong? By default, the following conditions are not exceptions: first, an end-of-file condition, which is only possible when reading from a file; and second, a no-record-found condition when an EGL record is the I/O object. In the following example, the defaults apply.

```
try
   get mySQLRecord;
   onException (except SQLException)
      ;
end
if (mySQLRecord is noRecordFound)
   ;
end
```

If you prefer to cause the end-of-file (endOfFile) and no-record-found (noRecordFound) conditions to be treated as exceptions, set the following program or handler annotation to *yes*: ThrowNrfEofExceptions.

CHAPTER 7

EGL Handlers for User Interface

In general, the word *handler* refers to logic that responds to an event. Some events are interactive; for example, a user's click of an onscreen button. Other events occur when a report is being formatted in memory, before the report is displayed or printed. For example, if a report is listing all corporate employees, one event is the completion of the list of sales people, at which point the report might include a subtotal.

In EGL, event handling is provided by functions in the EGL handler, which is a category of logic part. Our focus is on the handlers used with JavaServer Faces, BIRT reports, EGL text reporting, and, as mentioned in passing, Rich UI.

EGL JSF Handler

If you are using JavaServer Faces, an *EGL JSF handler* guides the user's interaction with a specific Web page. In most cases, you've *bound* each Web-page field to a variable in the EGL JSF handler, as illustrated in Figure 7.1.

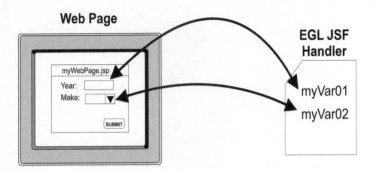

Figure 7.1: Web-Page Fields Bound to Variables in the EGL JSF Handler

The binding has two aspects. First, when the EGL JSF handler assigns a value to the variable, the JSF runtime ensures that the Web-page field receives the value. Second, when the user types data into the Web page and submits the content to the server, the JSF runtime ensures that the variable in the EGL JSF handler receives the new content from the Web-page field.

Validation is important to that second step. The JSF runtime can conduct a variety of tests on the user's input, from simple tests ("Does the value include only numeric digits?") to a range test ("Is the value between 50 and 100?"). Also possible is use of a validator function, which in this case is an EGL JSF handler function that determines whether a value conforms to a complex set of business rules. ("Is the user's payment up to date? If not, is the user's credit good enough to justify our sending the requested product?") In most cases, a failure of any of the tests causes a re-display of the same Web page, with an error message.

The EGL JSF handler oversees the interaction between user and code in another way. A Web-page button can be bound to a function in the EGL JSF handler. This binding means that at run time, when the user clicks that button, the function acts as an event handler, responding to the values received from the Web page into the variables, as illustrated in Figure 7.2.

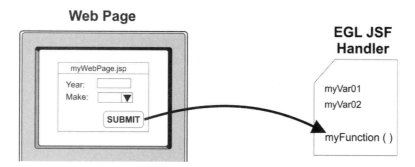

Figure 7.2: Web-Page Button Bound to a Function in the EGL JSF Handler

Similarly, a hypertext link in the Web page can be bound to a function in the EGL JSF handler, in which case a user's click of that link causes the function to be invoked.

Sample Handler

We'll describe how the EGL JSF handler interacts with the Web page shown in Figure 7.3.

Figure 7.3: Sample Web Page

Here's the related EGL JSF handler, myTestHandler.

```
Handler myTestHandler type JSFHandler
    { onConstructionFunction = onConstruction,
      onPrerenderFunction = onPrerender,
      scope = session,
      view = "myTestHandler.jsp" }

myInput01 InputType
    { ValidatorFunction = validate01, ValidationOrder = 2 };
myInput02 InputType
    { ValidatorFunction = validate02, ValidationOrder = 1 };
myTimestamp STRING;
const MASK STRING = "mm:ss:SSSS";
counter INT;
myOutput01, myOutput02, myOutput03 OutputType;

Function onConstruction()
    counter = 0;
end

Function onPrerender()
    counter = counter + 1;
end

Function validate01()
    wait(.02);
    myTimestamp = StrLib.formatTimeStamp
        (DateTimeLib.currentTimestamp(), MASK);
    myOutput01 = myTimestamp;
end

Function validate02()
    wait(.02);
    myTimestamp = StrLib.formatTimeStamp
        (DateTimeLib.currentTimestamp(), MASK);
    myOutput02 = myTimestamp;
end

Function respondToButtonClick()
    wait(.02);
    myTimestamp = StrLib.formatTimeStamp
        (DateTimeLib.currentTimestamp(), MASK);
    myOutput03 = myTimestamp;
end
```

Listing 7.1: EGL JSF Handler

We'll describe the handler's data and then the structure and logic.

Data in myTestHandler

In one of several scenarios for creating the page and handler, we define two
data items named InputType and OutputType.

```
dataItem InputType STRING
    {DisplayUse = input, DisplayName = "input: "}
end

dataItem OutputType STRING         .
    {DisplayUse = output, DisplayName = "output: "}
end
```

The annotation DisplayUse specifies the kind of Web-page control that will be
bound to the variable by default. The annotation DisplayName specifies a
default label for that control. Our intent is to create a binding between an input
text box and a variable of type InputType; and to create a binding between a
read-only text box and a variable of type OutputType.

In the JSF handler, the variables of type InputType have annotations beyond
those provided in the related data item. ValidatorFunction identifies a function
that determines whether the user input in a bound Web-page field is valid.
ValidationOrder indicates that the first Web-page field to be validated is the
field to which myInput02 is bound.

```
myInput01 InputType
    { ValidatorFunction = validate01, ValidationOrder = 2 };
myInput02 InputType
    { ValidatorFunction = validate02, ValidationOrder = 1 };
```

The variable myTimestamp and the constant MASK will help us show a
timestamp. The purpose is to demonstrate when different functions run.

```
myTimestamp STRING;
const MASK STRING = "mm:ss:SSSS";
```

The variable counter identifies how many times the handler transmits data to a
given user; and the variables of type OutputType display the values in
myTimestamp and counter.

```
counter INT;
myOutput01, myOutput02, myOutput03 OutputType;
```

Structure and Logic of myTestHandler

The EGL JSF handler annotations provide details that we'll explain only briefly for now: the onConstruction function runs when the user first requests the Web page; the onPrerender function runs every time that the user requests the Web page; the Scope annotation indicates how long the EGL JSF handler stays in memory on the Web application server; and the View annotation identifies (in essence) the Web page that runs under the handler's control. Chapter 8 includes a further explanation.

Now we'll outline the runtime events, assuming that the Web-page fields are bound to the appropriate variables and that the Web-page button is bound to the function respondToButtonClick. We'll describe the binding process soon.

When the handler first runs for a given user, the onConstruction function runs, setting counter to 0; and the onPrerender function runs, setting counter to 1. A Web page is displayed with the number 1 in the field that's bound to the counter variable. Here's the code.

```
Function onConstruction()
    counter = 0;
end

Function onPrerender()
    counter = counter + 1;
end
```

On seeing the Web page, the user may type data in one or both input fields, but the handler receives the input only when the user presses the button. For example, if the user changes no input fields and clicks the button, the following code runs immediately.

```
Function respondToButtonClick()
    wait(.02);
    myTimestamp = StrLib.formatTimeStamp
        (DateTimeLib.currentTimestamp(), MASK);
    myOutput03 = myTimestamp;
end
```

The effect of respondToButtonClick is to wait for 2 seconds, as necessary to ensure that the handler provides different values for different timestamps. The handler then sets myOutput03 with the current timestamp, which is formatted in accordance with the value of MASK. The onPrerender function runs, and the timestamp and counter value (now 2) are displayed.

Next, if the user types a value into the first and second input field and clicks the button, the validator functions run in the order specified in the ValidationOrder annotations. Here are the validator functions.

```
Function validate01()
    wait(.02);
    myTimestamp = StrLib.formatTimeStamp
        (DateTimeLib.currentTimestamp(), MASK);
    myOutput01 = myTimestamp;
end

Function validate02()
    wait(.02);
    myTimestamp = StrLib.formatTimeStamp
        (DateTimeLib.currentTimestamp(), MASK);
    myOutput02 = myTimestamp;
end
```

In general, the field-specific validator functions runs for all fields that the user changed, even if a specific validation fails. A validation fails if a validator function runs sysLib.setError; however, that function is not invoked in myTestHandler, and all validations succeed.

In our scenario, several functions now run, in the following order: validate02, validate01, respondToButtonClick, and onPrerender. The values provided to the user demonstrate the behavior.

Generation Outputs

The effect of generating the EGL JSF handler is to create several outputs, including these: first, the Java equivalent of the EGL JSF handler; second, a formatted but largely empty Web page, if the page doesn't already exist; and third, a set of entries in an onscreen area named the Page Data view.

The Page Data view makes data and function binding possible, including one entry for each global variable in the EGL JSF handler and one entry for each handler function, with a few exceptions. In our example, an entry is provided for seven variables and for the functions respondToButtonClick, validate01, and validate02 (Figure 7.4).

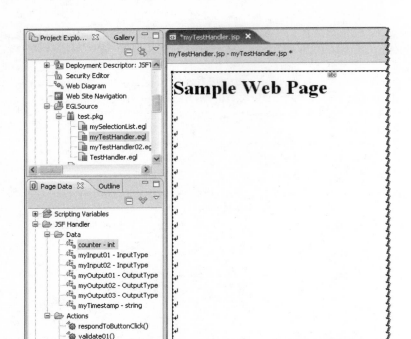

Figure 7.4: Page Data View Before Binding

Binding

The basic process for binding a Web-page field to a variable is that you drag an entry from the Page Data view and drop the entry on the Web-page surface (Figure 7.5). For data, the entry includes visual detail such as the type of control that you intended, as well as a default label. For actions—functions that you're providing—the entry lets you create a button that's bound to the specified function.

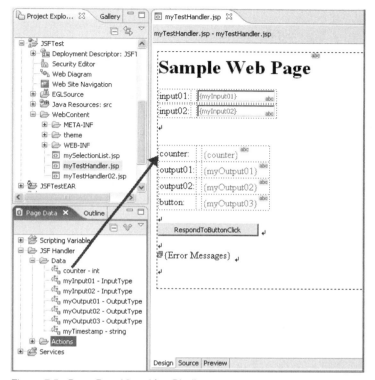

Figure 7.5: Page Data View After Binding

The importance of having up-to-date entries in the Page Data view explains why—by default—the RBD workbench generates an EGL JSF handler as soon as the handler is saved. However, immediate update of the Page Data view isn't necessary for everyone. You might send your work to a Web-page designer, who would use the entries in the Page Data view to format the Web page.

The person who binds a Web-page field to a variable can accept or overwrite details that were specified in the EGL JSF handler.

Support for BIRT Reports

Your EGL program can invoke the BIRT report engine, which is software that creates graphically sophisticated output. Figure 7.6 outlines the runtime relationships.

Figure 7.6: Support for BIRT Reports

Your code's initial access of the BIRT report engine can include the following details, among others:

- The name of a report design file, which identifies the structure of the report. You define the file in Rational Business Developer, in the BIRT Report Designer.

- The name of an output file, as well as the output type, which may be HTML or PDF.

- The name of an EGL BIRT handler.

The BIRT report engine interacts with the EGL BIRT handler, if any, and the handler in turn responds to runtime events. For example, the handler can receive displayable data from your EGL program and provide that data to the report engine as the engine prepares the report. For another example, the handler can change the color of report text in response to a value received into the report from your program or from a database or file.

Initial Access of the BIRT Report Engine

Your program accesses the report engine by creating a variable of type BIRTReport and then invoking functions that are available by way of that variable. Here's an example.

```
function CreateThisReport()

    myReport BIRTReport =
        new BIRTReport
            ("C:/MyReportDesign.rptdesign", null,
             "C:/MyFinalOutput.pdf", "pdf", null);

    myReport.createReportFromDesign();
end
```

The invocation of a function that creates the report—here, the function createReportFromDesign—is the last interaction between your program and the BIRT report engine. Thereafter, the report engine acts in accordance with the input you specify.

A BIRT handler is a variable based on the EGL BIRT handler part. To make the handler available to the report engine, you include the handler variable when you declare the BIRT report variable, as shown next.

```
function CreateThisReport draft Boolean)

    myHandler MyHandlerPart;

    myReport BIRTReport =
        new BIRTReport
            ("C:/MyReportDesign.rptdesign", null,
             "C:/MyFinalOutput.pdf", "pdf", myHandler);

    myReport.createReportFromDesign();
end
```

BIRT Handler

The BIRT handler is a generatable logic part that contains event handlers. For example, consider the following report table, which lists customers and the balance due for each.

Table 7-1: BIRT Report without Event Handling			
Last Name	**First Name**	**Account Balance**	**Remark**
Summer	Cleo	0	
Smith	Grace	42.00	
Taylor	Vlad	0	
Winter	Ben	22.00	

As the report is being prepared, the BIRT report engine invokes an event handler in response to each row created in the table. If an account balance is present, the event handler updates the row. Here's the same output when the event handler is in use.

Table 7-2: BIRT Report with Event Handling			
Last Name	**First Name**	**Account Balance**	**Remark**
Summer	Cleo	0	
Smith	Grace	42.00	Balance Due
Taylor	Vlad	0	
Winter	Ben	22.00	Balance Due

The following BIRT handler includes the function onMyLabel, which is the event hander for our example.

```
Handler MyHandlerPart type BIRTHandler

    function onMyLabel( myLabel LabelInstance,
                        myContext ReportContext )
        {   EventType = onCreate,
            ElementName = "remark" }

        myBalance float =
            myLabel.getRowData().getColumnValue("balance");
        if ( myBalance > 0 )
            myLabel.text = "Balance Due";
        end
    end
end
```

The name of any BIRT event handler is arbitrary. If the EventType annotation is set to onCreate, the event handler is invoked during creation of a particular kind of report element, which in this case is a label that the design file identifies as *remark*. That label is present in each row of our report table.

The first event-handler parameter accepts the label instance associated with a specific row and uses that label instance to access other data in the row. If the Account Balance column—identified in the design file as *balance*—has a positive value, the event handler assigns the string *Balance Due* to the *remark* label.

Our event handler does not use the function parameter of type ReportContext. That parameter lets you get or set a report parameter at run time. For example, an event handler invoked early in report creation might set a report parameter so that only those customers who live in a particular city are represented in the report.

Support for EGL Text Reporting

We turn now to EGL text reporting. When you create a report with this technology, a *basic handler* starts the report in response to being invoked by an EGL program. The handler then returns control to the program, which invokes additional handler functions for doing tasks such as transferring data to the handler or signaling that the input is complete. As the report is being created, a text-report engine—a variable declared in the handler—invokes other functions in the handler. Figure 7.7 illustrates the relationships.

Figure 7.7: EGL Text Reporting

The program-handler interaction is greater than in the case of BIRT reports, where almost all the EGL logic is in the BIRT handler.

We can best describe the handler by example. Consider the following EGL text report:

```
                                                  page 1

       Name                Position

       Grace               President
       Taylor              Treasurer
```

To create the report, the following program invokes functions that reside in a basic handler named MyReportHandler.

```
Program MyProgram

    myHandler MyReportHandler{};

    Function main()
        myHandler.myInitialization();
        myHandler.myInput("Grace", "President");
        myHandler.myInput("Taylor", "Treasurer");
        myHandler.myFinish();
    end
end
```

All of those function names are arbitrary, but you are likely to divide the runtime processing as shown there: initialize the report, submit input as needed, and finish the report. You are also likely to code global variables in the basic handler so that the data your program transfers is available when the EGL text-report engine invokes handler functions to create output. In our example, a global variable is based on the following Record part.

```
Record HandlerRecordPart
    name STRING;
    position STRING;
end
```

Here's an outline of the handler.

```
Handler MyReportHandler type BasicHandler

    textReport TextReport{};
    pageNumber INT;
    handlerRecord HandlerRecordPart;

    Function myInitialization() end
    Function myInput(name STRING, position STRING) end
    Function myHeaderFunction(myEvent textReportEvent) end
    Function myRowFunction(myEvent textReportEvent) end
    Function myFinish() end
end
```

A variable of type TextReport is the text-report engine. Two other global variables are also available: pageNumber, which is an integer to store the page number; and handlerRecord, a record based on the Record part described earlier. Two of the functions are accessed by the text-report engine: myHeaderFunction, which writes header details on each output page, and myRowFunction, which writes a given row. Again, those function names are arbitrary.

The function names become known to the text-report engine when you register them by way of the variable textReport, as shown in the initialization function,

```
Function myInitialization()
    textReport.onFirstPageHeaderListener = myHeaderFunction;
    textReport.onPageHeaderListener = myHeaderFunction;
    textReport.onEveryRowListener   = myRowFunction;
    textReport.setFirstHeaderLines(5);
    textReport.startReport("D:/temp/myOutput.txt",
            null,null,null,null, 20, null);
end
```

The initialization function also sets the number of lines at the top of the first header and directs the text-report engine to start report production and to use 20 lines per output page.

The function myInput accepts data from the program, assigns input to a global record, and requests the text-report engine to create output; in this case, to create the following rows: a header, if the report requires one at that point in processing; and a row of data.

```
Function myInput(name STRING, position STRING)
    handlerRecord.name = name;
    handlerRecord.position = position;
    textReport.outputToReport();
end
```

The function myHeaderFunction reveals a simple way to specify output: by a set of statements that establish a column position, write fixed-length text, and move to the next line in the report. Here's the function, which begins by retrieving the page number from textReport.

```
Function myHeaderFunction(myEvent textReportEvent)
    pageNumber = textReport.getPageNumber();
    textReport.column(60);
    textReport.printText("page ");
    textReport.printText(pageNumber);
    textReport.println();
    textReport.println();
    textReport.column(5);
    textReport.printText("Name");
    textReport.column(30);
    textReport.printText("Position");
    textReport.println();
end
```

The parameter of type textReportEvent is characteristic of event handlers in EGL text reporting. The parameter contains the state field, which indicates whether the function was called because the first row is being printed, because the last row is being printed, or for neither reason. The information lets you test a condition before doing special processing at the start or end of a report.

The function myRowFunction inserts data from the program into the report.

```
Function myRowFunction(myEvent textReportEvent)
    textReport.column(5);
    textReport.printText(handlerRecord.name);
    textReport.column(30);
    textReport.printText(handlerRecord.position);
    textReport.println();
end
```

Last, the function myFinish closes the report file :

```
Function myFinish()
    myReport.finishReport();
end
```

Rich UI Handlers

Two types of handlers make Rich UI possible. An *RUI handler* contains definitions of onscreen widgets—the word *controls* is less used here—and guides the user's interaction with those widgets. The RUI handler is said to provide a *view* or *front end* to a Rich UI application. In contrast, an *RUI model* is the local *back end* of a Rich UI application, as needed for business processing. In many cases, that local back end accesses remote services for the purpose of retrieving and storing data.

We give no further details on working with Rich UI because the technology is still emerging as this book is going to press. For up-to-date details, download the code that's available from the following Web site:

http://www.alphaworks.ibm.com/tech/reglrws

CHAPTER 8

EGL and JavaServer Faces

To build a modern software application, you need to understand where and when different actions occur. This chapter suggests a way of thinking about enterprise applications in general and describes the specific interplay of EGL-generated code and the JavaServer Faces runtime.

EGL and Web Applications

We'll start with a few words on what occurs at Web-application run time.

In response to a subset of requests, a server retrieves a local resource known as a *static Web page*—a file written in some variation of Hypertext Markup Language (HTML)—and transmits the content of that file to your browser. The term *static* indicates that the server did not insert additional data into the stream at run time; all the data came from the file. However, *static* does not mean *lacking capability*. A static Web page might provide multimedia content and might include *JavaScript*. JavaScript is code that runs in the browser; can respond instantaneously to user clicks without necessarily interacting with the server; and can retrieve business data from remote services.

The transmission of static Web pages does not involve much processing on the server. The use of static Web pages is characteristic of EGL Rich UI.

A server that's compliant with Java Enterprise Edition (JEE) can create and serve a *dynamic Web page*, which is HTML that's built at run time and can include data known only at run time; in particular, details retrieved from databases. As is true of static Web pages, dynamic Web pages might provide multimedia content, include JavaScript, and access services. However, the main processing tends to occur on the server.

Web-based processing fits into a larger mechanism for interacting with the user. In the description that follows, our focus is on EGL support for JavaServer Faces.

Logical Tiers at Run Time

A *tier* is software that fulfills a large and distinct purpose at run time. Consider, for example, the four-tier division illustrated in Figure 8.1.

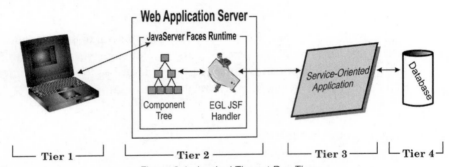

Figure 8.1: *Logical Tiers at Run Time*

Tier 1 is typically a Web browser. After the user requests a new Web page, the browser submits a request to the Web application server, receives and interprets HTML, and builds the user interface. The user then submits data from a business form that's embedded in the HTML.

Tier 2 is a Web application server. In the usual case, the server invokes logic on tier 3. The purpose might be to retrieve business data to be included in the HTML that will be returned to the browser. Another purpose might be to transmit the user's form data so that the data can be stored in a database.

Tier 3 is software that runs business-specific logic that in turn accesses enterprise databases. Increasingly, the business-specific logic is a service-oriented application, as described later.

Tier 4 corresponds to a database management system.

A single platform can fulfill some or all of the four roles: providing a browser, supporting a Web application server, providing services, and hosting one or more databases. The examples in this book assume that at development time, you have the convenience of having all four tiers on a single platform such as Windows XP.

Model, View, and Controller

An organizing idea in modern application development is that the following kinds of issues are handled separately: choices related to a user interface, and choices related to the data in persistent storage. In this section, we review the separation in a general way, without reference to a particular kind of technology. Our language is general because the technologies are so varied, but we'll follow up by noting how the separation applies to JavaServer Faces.

The back-end aspect of processing is the *Model*, which is defined in various ways: the business data found in persistent storage, the business data brought from persisent storage into a specific application, or the logic that accesses the data in persistent storage.

The front-end aspect of processing is the *View*, which is also defined in various ways: the business data received from and presented to the user, the overall mechanism by which data is exchanged with the user, or the visual characteristics of the user interface.

The separation of Model and View allows for a division of labor. A developer might handle database access and business-data manipulation while a Web-page designer focuses on the user interface. This division lets people fulfill a task appropriate to their training and lets different tasks proceed in parallel.

The *Controller* is the logic that oversees the interaction between the Model and View. The presence of this intermediate logic means that your organization can be more flexible, changing the View used to access a given Model and, less often, changing the Model used to provide data to a given View.

In relation to our description of logical tiers, the browser and to some extent the Web application server are the View, and the services that access the databases—along with the databases themselves—are the Model. The Controller is coded on the Web application server, primarily.

The notion of Model, View, and Controller (MVC) can affect the design of logic provided on a single tier, as shown next.

JavaServer Faces

One technique for developing Web applications quickly is to use a *framework*, which is a combination of runtime logic and a set of configuration files that affect the runtime behavior. A framework also includes constructs used at development time. An example of such a construct is the use of controls that are placed on a Web-page surface.

A framework can offer several benefits. First, it lets you write fewer lines of code. The framework handles the runtime situations that are common in most applications. Like other advances in software technology, the framework shields business developers from the complexity of runtime systems.

The framework also simplifies application update. To customize some behaviors of your application, you don't alter and recompile your code; instead, you customize text files for the framework, either in a text editor or by setting values in a graphical environment. We describe the situation by saying that the framework *externalizes logic*.

A framework's creators decide what the framework accomplishes, what application behavior is predetermined, and what application behavior is externalized. The cost of relying on their work is that you lose the ability to control some of the behavior yourself. However, a well-designed framework allows you to customize a lot, in which case the framework's benefits outweigh the cost.

In the next pages, we highlight the JavaServer Faces (JSF) framework. Our review of the JSF internals explains the runtime behavior of a server-centric, EGL-generated Web application. However, we omit some of the technical details of the JSF runtime. For the non-EGL details, see the *JavaServer Faces Specification Version 1.1* by Sun Microsystems, Inc., at the following Web site: *http://java.sun.com/javaee/javaserverfaces/download.html*.

Controller

The JavaServer Faces runtime controls a set of applications, including those provided by one or more EGL JSF handlers. You customize the JSF runtime largely by relying on Rational Business Developer, which automatically updates a configuration file being deployed with your application. The update involves two details that help to clarify how your EGL code interacts with the JSF runtime.

First, the configuration file identifies the runtime Java handler as a *managed bean*, which means that the JSF runtime can access your code as needed. Second, the configuration file includes navigation rules to specify what logic will be accessed when the JSF runtime receives a request. One request might be from a JSF handler function that issues an EGL forward statement to navigate to a new page. The forward statement might specify an outcome value such as success or failure, in which case the JSF runtime reviews the navigation rules and then invokes the runtime logic that you associated with the specified outcome value.

In your first work with EGL JSF handlers, you are likely to specify an outcome value that's identical to the name of the Web page you wish to invoke. If you follow that convention, you don't need to update the JSF configuration file by hand.

View

You build a JSF-compliant Web page. The page includes tags that correspond to controls such as text boxes and buttons. The JSF runtime uses the information in those tags to structure the HTML transmitted to the browser.

When you work with a JSP file in the RBD Page Designer, you can see the tags if you click on the Source tab. The tags are organized in a hierarchy. For example, a form tag (starting with <h:form>) might include an input tag (starting with <h:inputText>) and a button tag (starting with <hx:commandExButton>).

Consider the following input tag.

```
<h:inputText
    id="textMyInput011"
    value="#{myTestHandler.myInput01}"
    binding="#{myTestHandler.myInput01_Ref}"
    styleClass="inputText">
</h:inputText>
```

The id property holds the component ID, which is used in some EGL functions. The value property holds a JSF *value-binding expression*, which indicates that the Web-page field represented by the tag is bound to the handler field specified in curly braces. In this case, the managed-bean name in the JSF configuration file is myTestHandler; and the variable name in the JSF handler is myInput01. The binding property also includes a value-binding expression; but in this case, the property is solely for use by EGL system code. The styleClass property causes the Web-page field to have the visual characteristics of a text box used for input.

Another tag property of interest is the action property, which in many cases identifies an EGL JSF handler function. The action value identifies what logic to run in response to the user's click. The following action property results in the runtime invocation of the handler function respondToButtonClick.

```
action="#{myTestHandler.respondToButtonClick}"
```

The JSF runtime creates server-side *components*—Java objects in memory—that correspond to the JSF tags for a given Web page. A component includes tag-specific detail. A runtime hierarchy of components—the *JSF component tree*—corresponds to the tag hierarchy that you see at development time. The tree is illustrated in Figure 8.2.

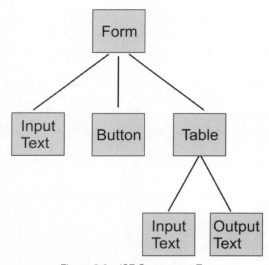

Figure 8.2: JSF Component Tree

An EGL JSF handler can update aspects of the components in response to user input or back-end processing. For example, the handler can do any of the following tasks: change the style of a textbox; change the target of a hypertext link; enable or disable a control; change the size of an image; assign different colors to alternate rows in an onscreen table; or add JavaScript to a button so that a user click causes processing in the browser.

The JSF runtime *renders* the component tree; in other words, creates HTML that represents the content of the tree. The JSF runtime then transmits the HTML to the user.

The component tree and the rendered HTML are the View.

Model

In relation to JavaServer Faces, the Model is the global data in the EGL JSF handler. A managed bean—the EGL JSF handler—is created, updated, or destroyed in accordance with a set of rules that we describe later.

The JSF runtime assigns the EGL JSF handler to one of three *scopes*, each of which defines the lifetime of a managed bean. The scopes correspond to the three possible values of the Scope annotation: *request*, *session*, and *application*. The three scopes are available to you, as well, allowing for temporary storage as you transfer data from one function to another in the same or a different EGL JSF handler. We speak of running an EGL JSF handler or storing data "in scope":

- *Request scope* is available from the time that the JSF runtime receives a request from the user until your code responds to that user. An EGL JSF handler in request scope might provide the status of a specific order in response to a user request. You can store data in request scope regardless of the Scope annotation.

- *Session scope* is available from the time that the JSF runtime receives data from the user and lasts through multiple user-code interactions until the server session is made invalid. The server session is made invalid in several ways: for example, by a session timeout or because the EGL JSF handler is *restarted*—reinitialized—in the Web application server. A handler in session scope might hold an order number required for a series of interactions. You can store data in session scope when the Scope annotation is *session* or *application*.

- *Application scope* is a multiple-user scope and is available from the time a Web application starts for any user and lasts until the application is terminated. An EGL JSF handler in application scope might hold the next available order number. You can store data in application scope when the Scope annotation is *application*. Use of application scope is an advanced subject, and we'll not consider the issue again.

JSF Life Cycle

When a user requests a page or submits form data, or when some logic forwards control to a JSF handler, the initial phase of the JSF life cycle begins.

Figure 8.3 illustrates the JSF life cycle and reflects EGL-specific behaviors.

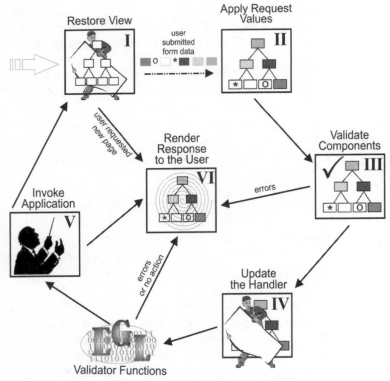

Figure 8.3: JSF Life Cycle with EGL

Overview

The JSF runtime creates the component tree; analyzes whether the user's form data, if any, is valid; and acts in one of two ways. If the user submitted invalid form data, the JSF runtime renders the component tree and displays the page again so that the user can correct and resubmit the input. Alternatively, if the user's input is valid, the JSF runtime updates the Model—the data values in the EGL JSF handler—and continues processing in accordance with the intended application flow, possibly forwarding control to another Web page.

JSF Life-Cycle Phases

We now consider the JSF life-cycle phases.

Phase I: Restore View. The JSF runtime creates the component tree and determines whether the EGL JSF handler exists. At this point, a handler intended for request scope cannot exist, and a handler intended for session scope may or may not exist, depending on what events preceded Phase I.

If the handler does not exist, the JSF runtime creates the handler, places it in the scope specified in the JSF configuration file, and runs the onConstruction function to provide data to the component tree.

If the user requested the page and did not submit form data, or if the page received control from other logic such as another EGL JSF handler, processing continues at Phase VI: Render Response. Alternatively, if the user submitted form data, processing continues at Phase II.

In later phases, the EGL JSF handler may be removed from scope. The effect of removing a handler from scope is that the handler will be destroyed, and a later use of the same handler will display fresh data to the user.

Phase II: Apply Request Values. Each component receives whatever data was provided by the page control that corresponds to the component.

Phase III: Process Validations. The JSF runtime converts the input strings to the Java data types that are required by the EGL JSF handler. Then, for each component in turn, the JSF runtime handles both EGL and JSF validations.

Process Validations is when most validations occur for each component. You specify the JSF validations, if any, when you work on the JSP file in the Page

Designer. You specify the EGL validations when you write the EGL JSF handler.

All components are validated. For a given component, the conversions and validations occur until one of them fails. You cannot specify the order of component validations in Phase III.

The EGL component-specific validations include elementary edits such as minimum input; type-based edits such as digits only; and comparisons against data-table values. After the EGL and JSF validations run for a specific component, the EGL onValueChange function runs for the same component. Other EGL validator functions run in a later phase.

If a conversion or validation fails during Phase III, as occurs if an onValueChange function issues sysLib.setError, processing continues at Phase VI: Render Response. Otherwise, processing continues at Phase IV.

Phase IV: Update the Handler. The JSF runtime updates the EGL JSF handler with the validated data. The JSF specification refers to this phase as **Update Model Values**.

Phase V: Invoke Application. During this phase, the JSF runtime responds to the action requested by the user. From the perspective of JavaServer Faces, the code that's executed is "the application" because phase V is when business logic runs.

Before the JSF runtime fulfills the action specified by the user, the JSF runtime runs all the component-specific EGL validator functions, even if some fail.

The default order of validator-function execution is based on the position of tags on the Web page: left to right, primarily, and top to bottom. You can override that order by specifying the EGL ValidationOrder annotation for some or all components.

If all validations succeed, the JSF runtime runs the EGL validator function for the handler as a whole.

If a validation function runs sysLib.setError or if the user specified no action value, processing continues at Phase VI. However, if all validations succeed, the JSF runtime responds to the binding expression in the action property of the SUBMIT button, as found in the JSP file that represents the Web page. In most cases, the binding expression specifies a handler function, which can update the component tree, forward control to another Web page, or do other work.

An EGL forward statement ends processing in the handler. If the handler is in request scope, the handler is removed from that scope. If the handler is in session scope, the handler is removed from that scope only if the annotation cancelOnPageTransition was set to true and only if the forward statement directs processing to a handler other than the current handler.

Phase VI: Render Response to the User. The JSF runtime runs the onPrerender function, renders the component tree, transmits the response, and runs the handler's onPostrender function. Any change to the component tree in the onPostrender function affects the user only if the same page is rerendered later.

If the handler is in request scope, the JSF runtime removes the handler from request scope; and any change to the component tree in the onPostrender function has no effect.

CHAPTER 9

EGL and Service-Oriented Architecture

This chapter outlines EGL support for service-oriented architecture (SOA). A later tutorial gives a practical review.

Overview of SOA

(Some material in this section first appeared in *SOA for the Business Developer: Concepts, BPEL, and SCA*, published by MC Press: *http://www.mc-store.com/5079.html*.)

SOA is a way of organizing software. The technology is based on *services*, which are customized units of software that run in a network. A service

- Handles a business process such as calculating an insurance quote or distributing email, or handles a relatively technical task such as accessing a database, or provides business data and the technical details needed to construct a graphical interface

- Can access another service and, with the appropriate runtime technology, can access a traditional program and respond to different kinds of requesters—for example, to Web applications

- Is relatively independent of other software so that changes to a requester require few or no changes to the service, while changes to the internal logic of a service require few or no changes to the requester

The relative independence of the service and other software is called *loose coupling*. The flexibility offered by loose coupling protects your company from excessive costs when business or technical requirements change.

A service can handle interactions within your organization, as well as between your organization and its suppliers, partners, and customers. The location of a requester can be anywhere in the world. However, security or technical constraints can make access to a service impossible for a given requester.

Service Location

The location of a service is set when the service is deployed. When is the location known to the requester?

- The details on service location can be embedded in the business logic of the requester, but that usage is inflexible. If the service location changes, the requester must be recompiled and redeployed.

- In most cases, the details on service location are provided by configuration files at the site where the requester is deployed. That usage is more flexible because the configuration files can change during the years when the requester is in use, and the requester can access the service even if the service is deployed to a new location.

- In some cases, location details are passed to the requester at run time. That usage is flexible but adds complexity that is not required for most purposes.

Regardless of which of those cases applies, the developer can write the business logic so that the requester accesses one service rather than another in response to a runtime condition.

Migration of Existing Applications

SOA isn't only for new code. Migration of existing applications is especially appropriate in the following cases:

- The applications are monolithic, combining the logic of user interface, business processing, and data access, with update of one kind of logic requiring that your organization test multiple kinds of behavior.

- The applications are hard to understand—first, because the logic is monolithic, but second, because logic was repeatedly patched rather than rewritten as requirements changed. Updates take extra time as developers try to decipher the logic, and as the complexity grows, additional errors accompany updates.

- The application inventory has duplicate logic. Requests for change are unnecessarily disruptive, requiring changes in several places.

A Style of Development

SOA implies a style of development, with concern for the business as a whole and with an increased focus on modularity and reuse. From the developer's point of view, a change to a service orientation is only a change in emphasis, and many aspects of the development task are unaffected.

Structure of a Service-Oriented Application

A *service-oriented application* is an application composed largely of services. Often, the invoked services are in a hierarchy, as Figure 9.1 illustrates.

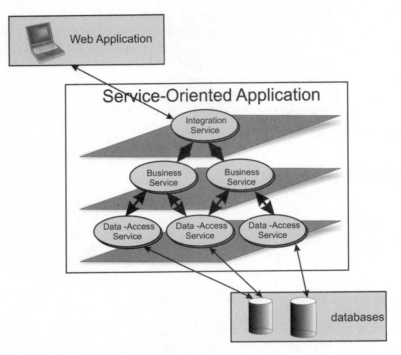

Figure 9.1: Service-Oriented Application

The topmost level contains one or more *integration services*, each of which controls a flow of activities such as processing an applicant's request for insurance coverage. Each integration service invokes one or more business services.

The second level is composed of services that each fulfill a relatively low-level business task. For example, an integration service might invoke a series of *business services* to verify the details provided by an insurance-policy applicant. If the business services return a set of values that are judged to mean "issue a policy," the integration service invokes yet another business service, which calculates a quote and returns the quote to the software that invoked the service-oriented application.

The third level consists of *data-access services*, each of which handles the relatively technical task of reading from and writing to data-storage areas such as databases and message queues. A data-access service is most often invoked from the business layer, but the easy access of services allows for different uses; for example, a requester such as a Web application can access a data-access service to assign initial values in a form.

Great complexity is possible. Some integration services provide different operations to different requesters, and some invoke other integration services. In addition, a requester might access different kinds of services from *within* a service-oriented application. The requester might access an integration service at one point and a business service at another.

EGL Support for Services

As noted in the Introduction, a service written in EGL can be deployed as an EGL service or a Web service. An EGL service exchanges data in a proprietary format, provides better performance, and can be deployed on any EGL target platform. A Web service exchanges data in a text-based format, is widely accessible, and can be deployed only on a Web application server or on CICS.

We described the EGL Service and Interface parts in Chapter 3 and showed that a variable declaration provided access to the service, as in the following example.

```
Program myProgram

   Function main()
     myInterface myInterfacePart
        {
            @BindService
                {bindingKey = "myInterfacePart"}
        };
     myEmployee STRING = myInterface.getEmployee("910");
     sysLib.writeStdOut(myEmployee);
   end
end
```

The BindService annotation identifies an entry in the EGL deployment descriptor.

EGL Deployment Descriptor

The EGL deployment descriptor is a development-time file that stores information on two different issues: the services your code is requesting, and the characteristics of the services being generated.

The deployment descriptor is an input to the EGL generator and, by default, the output is generated when you save the file. The nature of the output varies. In every case, the output facilitates the transport of data to and from a service.

Service Client Bindings

If your EGL source code requests a service, you specify access details for the service in the EGL deployment descriptor. The access details are in a section of the deployment descriptor reserved for *service client bindings*. You specify one of three types of bindings: an EGL binding, to access an EGL service; a native binding, to access a service program that runs on IBM i; or a Web binding, to access a Web service, regardless of whether the service was generated by EGL.

System functions in the EGL serviceLib library let an EGL-generated requester retrieve and set binding information. For example, your code can direct processing to a different version of a service in response to a runtime condition. One version of a service might be appropriate for a user who needs access to confidential data or is paying a premium.

Web Deployment

If the generated output will be deployed as a Web service, the EGL generator uses the deployment descriptor to create a configuration file known as a Web Services Description Language (WSDL) file. The WSDL file includes details on the service location, as well as on the runtime interface—the operations provided by the service, as well as the parameters and return values for each operation. You include the WSDL file with the other content you deploy to a Web application server. You also make the WSDL file available in some way—perhaps in a repository—so that the file can be deployed with the code that requests access to the service.

Web-Service Access

If your EGL source code is accessing a Web service, the service provider makes available a WSDL file that represents the location and interface details for that service. When you work with the RBD deployment descriptor editor, you can accept the WSDL file as input, and RBD provides an Interface part. You can use the Interface part as the basis of a variable in your code, and the variable provides access to the operations in the service.

An important point is that the service-location details are not embedded in the business logic of your code, but are present externally in the WSDL file. The service-location details may change over the years, but you don't need to regenerate or recompile your code in response to the change.

In a small number of cases, you won't use the deployment descriptor editor to create an Interface part when you're preparing to access a Web service. If the service is itself written in EGL, you can use the related EGL Service part as the basis of a variable in your code.

When an Interface Part is Not What You Expect

As you try out Rational Business Developer in your workstation, you may find yourself working with an Interface part that has characteristics that are different from what you expect. The situation can occur if you do as follows:

1. Generate an EGL Service part to be deployed as a Web service; and in this way, create a WSDL file

2. Use Rational Business Developer to derive an EGL Interface part from the WSDL file

For example, here's myService, an EGL Service part.

```
Service myService
  Function step01 (outInt INT OUT, inInt INT INOUT)
    ;
  end
end
```

Here's an EGL Interface part that was derived from a WSDL file that was itself derived from myService.

```
Interface myService
  Function step01 (inInt INT INOUT, outInt INT OUT);
end
```

The parameters in the second function signature are reversed, not because of an error, but because of a difference in how two different kinds of runtime software operate.

Here's what you need to know:

- When you're writing EGL-generated code to access a Web service that was written in EGL, you have complete flexibility in relation to how to define the variable being used to access the service. You can use the EGL Service part as the basis of the access variable. Also, you can use an EGL Interface part as the basis of the access variable, no matter how you derived the Interface part.

- When you're writing EGL-generated code to access an EGL service that is not deployed as a Web service, you have almost as much flexibility. You can use the EGL Service part as the basis of the access variable. Also, you can use an EGL Interface part as the basis of the access variable, if the Interface part was derived from the Service part. The only issue is the potential mismatch of function parameters if you use an EGL Interface part that was derived from a WSDL file.

You may encounter the issue when you're learning the product, but the case is unlikely to occur when you're writing enterprise applications.

CHAPTER 10

Introduction to the RBD Workbench

This chapter further describes the interactive environment where you'll create and debug EGL-based applications.

Welcome

When you first open IBM Rational Business Developer, you're asked to specify a *workspace*, which is a directory that stores the files specific to your development tasks (Figure 10.1).

Figure 10.1: Workspace Launcher

You're likely to use a single workspace as you fulfill a development effort. However, over time you're likely to use multiple workspaces and, in some cases, to switch from one workspace to another.

After you press OK at the Workspace Launcher, the workbench opens to a Welcome page, where you can move your cursor over icons that offer tutorials, samples, and other introductory material (Figure 10.2).

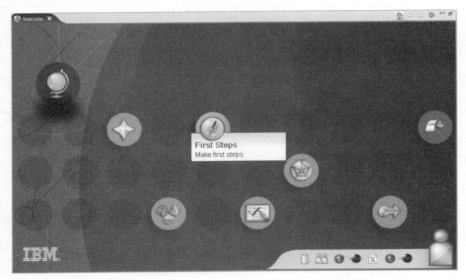

Figure 10.2: Welcome page

After you click an icon, you'll see the other icons at the top of the displayed page, and you can navigate from one kind of presentation to another (Figure 10.3).

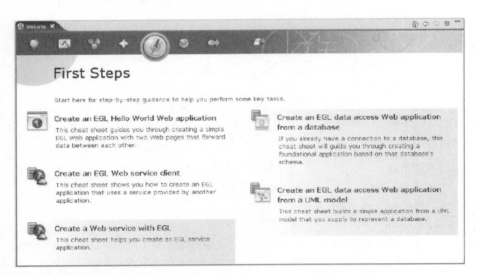

Figure 10.3: First Steps

To start your development work, close the Welcome. You can return later by clicking the Help menu, which offers extensive assistance, including quick-reference instructions called *cheat sheets* (Figure 10.4).

Figure 10.4: Cheat Sheet Selection

Preferences

One of your first and sometimes repeated tasks is to set up preferences. After you're at the Preferences dialog (**Window > Preferences**), you have many choices, and we'll highlight a few.

Capabilities

RBD lets you specify what product capabilities are available to you. By selecting only a subset of capabilities, you ensure that your experience is simpler and that the product's responsiveness is greater.

You can see the options by clicking **General > Capabilities** (Figure 10.5).

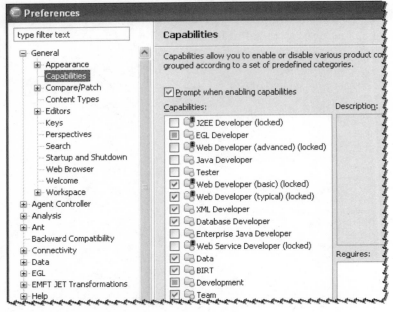

Figure 10.5: Capabilities

If a check box for a given capability is selected, that capability is fully present in the workbench. If a check box for a given capability is filled, the capability is present only in part. If a check box is not selected, the capability was installed but is not now available.

If you start working with a technology that you haven't used before and find that you're unable to do simple tasks, look into the capabilities. You may solve the problem by selecting a check box.

Web Browser

You can use a particular browser for all your Web-related work or can try a browser temporarily to see the effect of your choice at run time. To see or change the browser in use, click **General > Web Browser**.

EGL

The **EGL** preferences set defaults for the language editor and debugger and for other development-time functions. In the EGL **Editor** preferences, you can update the code templates available to your organization. For example, you can update the **try onException** template to include **SQLException**. The effect is to include **SQLException** as a default whenever a developer uses the template to create initial source code.

A particularly important EGL preference is **SQL Database Connections**. The purpose is to specify connection detail for development time. You can reuse your work when you specify connection detail for generation time and, in some cases, when you specify the detail for run time.

Views and Perspectives

Almost all your development work occurs in a *view*, which is an onscreen rectangle where a particular kind of interaction is available. You might type code in an editor view or drag a Web control from a palette view.

A *perspective* is a related set of views, along with a characteristic set of tool bars and menu items. In many cases, as you move from one kind of task to a different kind of task, you switch perspectives. You can customize a perspective, selecting what views to include, and can reset a perspective so that its default views are restored.

To open a new perspective, click **Window > Open Perspective** (Figure 10.6).

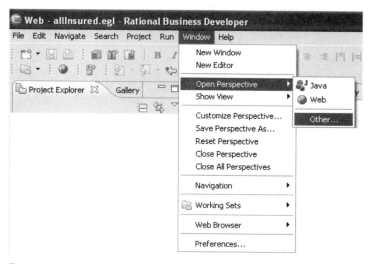

Figure 10.6: Open Perspective using the menu

The Workbench shows a set of icons for the perspectives you used previously. You can right-click the icons and select **Dock On** to place them at a different onscreen location. Also, you can left-click a particular icon to switch to a previously used perspective (Figure 10.7).

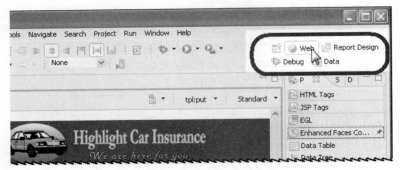

Figure 10.7: Select a Previously Used Perspective

To add a view to the current perspective, click **Window > Show View** (Figure 10.8).

Figure 10.8: Show View

In the next chapter, we show how to organize your work and how to fulfill a development effort that involves services and a Web application.

CHAPTER **11**

Tutorial

T his chapter describes how to create EGL source code in Rational
Business Developer and gives necessary background information.

The applications created here are for use by an insurance agent who works for
Highlight Insurance, a fictional company. At a technical level, the outcome of
the work is a Web application that accesses a service-oriented application in
two ways (Figure 11.1).

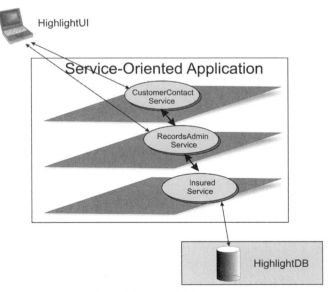

Figure 11.1: Tutorial Outcome

Projects

A *project* in RBD is a collection of files that represent a defined subset of a development effort. We'll demonstrate what a project is by working with four of them (Figure 11.2).

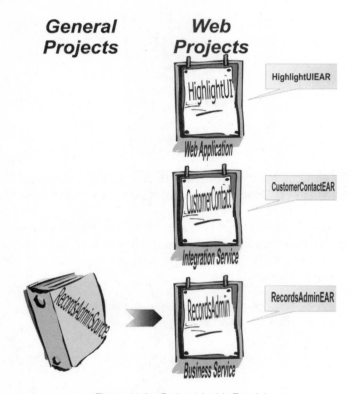

General Projects   **Web Projects**

Figure 11.2: Projects in this Tutorial

The projects are as follows:

- The Web project **HighlightUI** holds the EGL and Java files for a Web application

- The Web project CustomerContact holds the EGL and Java files for **CustomerContactService**, an integration service.

- The Web project **RecordsAdmin** holds the Java files for **RecordsAdminService**, a business service, and for **InsuredService**, a data-access service

- The General project **RecordAdminsSource** holds only the EGL files for the business and data-access services

Each of the three Web projects provides an Enterprise Archive (EAR) file for deployment. We'll describe that kind of file later.

To provide the data-access services quickly, we'll use the RBD Data Access Application Wizard. The wizard accepts details on the structure of database tables and then creates services that create, read, update, and delete table rows.

Even as we make the tutorial easier by using the wizard, we make the tutorial more difficult by using a project that holds only source code. If several people in your organization are developing code for a single application, each might work in a developer-specific source-code project and periodically generate output to a common project that holds only the deployable code. Also, you might need to generate the same code into different deployable projects—for example, one to support Apache Tomcat and one to support WebSphere Application Server. The tutorial shows you how to generate output into a project separate from your source code and helps you to understand some of the tasks that RBD handles for you in the usual case, when a single project includes both source code and generated output.

Prepare the Environment

If you want to work through the steps in this tutorial, do as follows.

1. If necessary, download Rational Business Developer—including WebSphere Application Server 6.1—for a 60-day trial period. You can access the software from the following site:

   http://www.ibm.com/developerworks/rational/products/rbde

2. Download HighlightDB, a small Derby database, from MC Press:

   http://www.mc-store.com/5087.html

   Please review that site for any additional instructions for this chapter.

3. Extract the zip file to C:\databases.

Please be aware that the version of Derby provided with Rational Business Developer allows only one connection at a given time and is primarily for running tutorials and testing simple applications. For information on Derby, see the following Web site, which also has details on upgrading to a more powerful verion:

http://db.apache.org/derby

Setup Internet Explorer

The tutorial assumes that you've installed WebSphere Application Server v6.1, which is included with Rational Business Developer. The tutorial also assumes that you're using the product's internal browser—Internet Explorer—and that the browser checks for new versions of a page during every user request. To make sure the browser is ready:

1. Open Internet Explorer outside of Rational Business Developer.

2. Click **Tools > Internet Options**. The Internet Options page is displayed.

3. If you're using Internet Explorer 6.x, the General tab includes an area devoted to Temporary Internet Files. Click **Settings**. At the Settings page, ensure that the following option is selected: **Every visit to the page**.

4. If you are using Internet Explorer 7.x, the General tab includes an area devoted to Browser History. Click **Settings**. At the **Temporary Internet Files and History Settings** page, ensure that the following option is selected: **Every time I visit the webpage**.

5. Click **OK** and, at the Internet Options page, click **OK**.

Machine Name and Port Number

Your Web application may be unable to invoke a Web service until you update a preference setting in the RBD Workbench. We'll give you an overview of the issue now and specify the keystroke details later.

Your copy of WebSphere Application Server "listens" for incoming Web-page requests and Web-service requests at a single *port*, which is always an address that's internal to the machine that hosts the server. In many cases, when you're working with your own copy of WebSphere Application Server, you can access pages and services by referring to the machine name *localhost* and the port number *9080*. However, *localhost:9080* is not always correct.

The EGL generator needs to know the correct machine name and port number. Otherwise, when the generator creates a Web service, the access details in the generated WSDL file will be wrong. The effect of wrong access details is seen after generation, when a requester—for example, the tutorial's Web application—uses the details in the WSDL file as a guide. If the details are wrong at run time (even in the development environment), the request fails.

How can you learn the machine name and port number used by WebSphere Application Server in RBD? The easiest answer is related to Web *pages*, not Web services.

When you work with Rational Business Developer, a particular set of clicks (**Run as > Run on Server**) causes the server to present a Web page. The server acts as if you had typed a Web address into a browser.

At the time of Web-page display, the machine name and port number of the server is in the Web-page address displayed at the browser. You can copy those details into the EGL preference that's used at the time of Web-service generation.

In short, to learn the machine name and port number to be included in an EGL-generated WSDL file, you'll develop a Web page for display.

Create the Web Application

To create the project HighlightUI:

1. In the Project Explorer, right-click a blank area

2. Click **New > Project** and, at the **New Project** dialog, expand **EGL**

3. Click **EGL Project**, then **Next;** alternatively, double-click **EGL Project**. The **New EGL Project** page is displayed.

4. Type the Project name as follows: **HighlightUI**

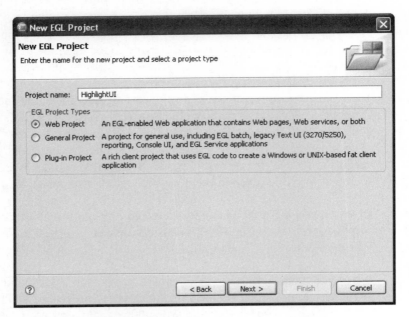

Figure 11.3: New EGL Project Wizard

5. Click **Web Project**.

6. Click **Next**, and under **Target Runtime**, accept **WebSphere Application Server v6.1**

7. Click **Finish**.

Start the Server

If the server is not started, do as follows:

1. In the Servers view at the bottom of Rational Business Developer, right-click **WebSphere Application Server v6.1**.

2. Click **Start**. Hereafter, start the server by clicking the Start icon, which is a white triangle embedded in a green circle.

3. If the server does not start, you may have a security issue. Right-click **WebSphere Application Server v6.1** and click **Open**. At the **Server Overview** page, under **Server Connection Type and admin port**, click **SOAP**. Save the file and start the server.

Explore the File Structure of a Web Project

At the left is the Project Explorer, which is a view that shows each project as the root of a tree. If you expand **HighlightUI**, you'll see the EGLSource folder. In your work with EGL, you'll create packages within the EGLSource folder; and within each package, EGL source files.

Let's take a look at the special file structure of a Web project:

1. The first entry under **HighlightUI** is **Deployment Descriptor: HighlightUI**. This entry provides access to one of the three types of deployment descriptors mentioned in this book: the Web deployment descriptor web.xml. The file establishes characteristics of the runtime environment and includes identifiers that refer to external resources such as databases.

2. Expand **WebContent**. The WebContent folder includes all the files that will be deployed as a Web Archive (WAR) file. A WAR file is a compressed file collection similar to a zip file. Rational Business Developer creates the WAR file when you export your work for deployment to a Web application server.

   The top of the WebContent folder is is now empty but will include HTML files, JavaServer Page files, or both; in essence, the Web pages. The META-INF folder holds files that describe the application content to the Web application server. And the theme folder holds cascading style sheets that control visual aspects of the runtime presentation, along with subfolders with files to provide whatever graphics, video, and music are being transmitted with the HTML.

   The WEB-INF directory holds configuration files that are specific to your application. In particular, the directory holds web.xml, which you were able to access easily in a previous step. Also in the WEB-INF directory are the classes and lib directories, which include your application logic.

3. Expand **HighlightUIEAR**. That project provides the details necessary to create an Enterprise Archive (EAR) file. The EAR file is another compressed file collection. The EAR file is created at Web-project creation if you indicated that the target server is WebSphere Application Server, which is JEE compliant. The EAR file is not created if you indicated that the target platform is Apache Tomcat, which does not handle these kind of files.

The EAR file can include WAR files and other deployable logic; for example, Java Archive (JAR) files, which are primarily collections of the Java class files required at deployment time.

The first entry in HighlightUIEAR gives you easy access to the EAR deployment descriptor file application.xml. That file can associate the resource identifiers—as specified in the WAR file—with runtime locations. We'll use such an identifier later.

As used at deployment time, the project structure helps to create the relationships needed to ensure that at run time, the Web application server seeks a file or database from the appropriate location.

Create the Web Page

We'll create a Web page in the RBD Page Designer, including a single header line. Later, we'll add controls and bind them to variables in the EGL JSF handler. This order of events is opposite to the procedure in Chapter 6, when we created the JSF handler first. The product accommodates either order.

To create the Web page:

1. In the Project Explorer, right-click **HighlightUI**.

2. Click **New > Web Page**.

3. At the Web page dialog, type **allInsured.jsp**. Make sure you specify the extension **.jsp**; otherwise, an HTML file is created.

4. In the Templates area of the dialog, expand **Sample Templates** and **Family A (no navigation)**.

5. Select a template, Clear the box for **Link page to template**, and click **Finish**. The Page Designer is displayed.

6. Select the string *Place your page content here*; type the string **List of Insured**; and create space for Web-page controls by pressing **ENTER** eight times.

7. Select **List of Insured**, right-click, and click **Properties**.

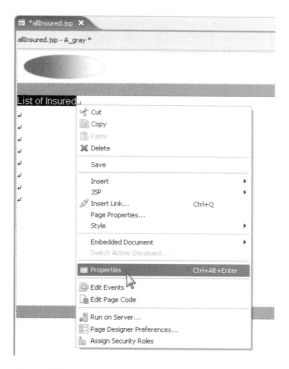

Figure 11.4: Properties menu

8. Ensure that **Text** is selected at the left of the Properties view, At the drop-down list for Paragraph, select **Heading 1**.

9. Save the file (press **Ctrl+s**—that is, hold down the **Ctrl** key and press **S**—or click **File** > **Save**). Do not close the JSP file.

View the EGL JSF Handler and Generate Output

To view the created EGL JSF handler:

1. Right click the Web-page surface and click **Edit Page Code**. The JSF handler named **allInsured.egl** is now available in the EGL editor.

```
package jsfhandlers;

handler allInsured type JSFHandler
    { onstructionFunction = onConstruction,
      onPrerenderFunction = onPrerender,
      view = "allInsured.jsp"}
    // Function Declarations
    function onConstruction()
    end
    function onPrerender()
    end
end
```

   RBD has created an EGL file with the same name as the JSP file, placed it under folder EGLSource and, within that folder, in the package **jsfhandlers**.

2. Close the file **allInsured.egl**.

3. To create a managed bean for use by the JSF runtime, go to the Project Explorer view, right-click **HighlightUI**, and click **Generate**.

Run the Web page

To run the Web page:

1. Place the cursor in the file **allInsured.jsp**

2. Go to the Project Explorer, which is at the left. At the tool bar at the top of that view, click the Link Editor icon, which has two arrows. The file **allInsured.jsp** is now highlighted. Hereafter, whatever file you're working on in Page Designer or EGL editor will be highlighted in Project Explorer.

The Link Editor icon toggles between two states: linking the views in the way just described, or unlinking them. When you want to change the linking behavior, click the icon.

3. In Project Explorer, right-click **allInsured.jsp** and then click **Run As > Run on Server**.

4. At the Define a New Server page, click **WebSphere Application Server v6.1**, check **Set server as project default**, and click **Finish**

5. A progress bar at the bottom right indicates that the project is *publishing*—being made available—to WebSphere Application Server. The Web page is displayed or, in some cases, an error Web page is displayed.

6. In either case, review the address bar at the top of the Web page. In most cases, the address is *http://localhost:9080/HighlightUI/allInsured.faces*, where *localhost* refers to the machine, *9080* is the port number, *HighlightUI* is the project name, *allInsured* is the JSP file name, and the extension *.faces* indicates that the page is running under the JSF runtime.

7. If the address does not include the precise string *localhost:9080*, click **Window > Preferences**. At the **Preferences** page, expand **EGL** and click **Service**. Then assign the machine name and port number. Those details will be used later, when we generate WSDL files for the services being deployed as Web services. Click **OK** (Figure 11.5).

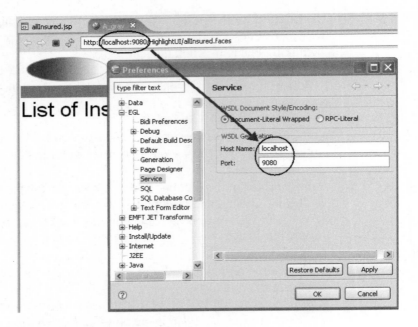

Figure 11.5: *Machine Name and Port Number*

8. If your Web page did not display successfully, reset your environment by removing the Web-application EAR file from the server:

    a. Go to the Servers view at the bottom of Rational Business Developer and right-click **WebSphere Application Server v6.1**.

    b. Select **Add and Remove Projects**.

    c. At the **Add and Remove Projects** page, click **Remove All**, then **Finish**.

    d. In Project Explorer, right-click **allInsured.jsp** and then click **Run As > Run on Server**.

9. Close the browser.

Create the Data-Access Services

We'll create the project RecordsAdminSource and then use the Data Access
Application Wizard to define a database connection and create data-access
services.

To open the EGL perspective (Figure 11.6):

1. Click **Window > Open Perspective > Other > EGL**

2. Click **OK**

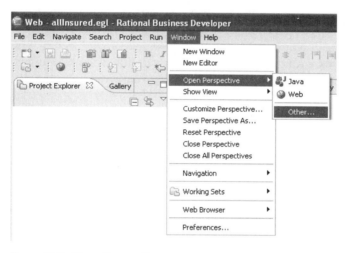

Figure 11.6: Open Perspective

Create the Project RecordsAdminSource

To create the project RecordsAdminSource:

1. In the Project Explorer, right-click a blank area.

2. Click **New > Project** and, at the New Project dialog, expand **EGL**
   and double-click **EGL Project**. The **New EGL Project** page is
   displayed. A General Project is appropriate for most EGL projects
   other than those used to create Web-based code.

3. Type the Project name **RecordsAdminSource** and click **General Project**. Click **Next**, then **Finish**.

Launch the EGL Data Access Application Wizard

To launch the EGL Data Access Application wizard:

1. In the Project Explorer, expand **RecordsAdminSource**.

2. Right-click **EGLSource**, then click **New > Other**.

3. Expand **EGL** and double-click **EGL Data Access Application**.

4. At Project Name, select the project to receive the wizard's output: **RecordsAdminSource**. We can now define a database connection, which will be valid throughout the current workspace.

5. Click **New** to display the **New Connection** page.

6. Make sure that the following entry is checked: **Use default naming convention**. The connection name will be created for you.

7. Expand **Derby** and choose **10.1** from the list. The JDBC driver changes to represent that selection.

8. Next to Database location, click **Browse** and navigate to the database location: c:\databases\HighlightDB. Click **OK**. The connection name changes to the name of the database.

9. Next to Class location, click **Browse** and navigate to your product installation directory and then to the JDBC Driver Class file, derby.jar. This file is likely to be in the following location: *<RBDInstallDir>*\runtimes\base_v61\derby\lib, where *<RDBInstallDir>* is probably C:\Program Files\IBM\SDP70. Double-click the file name derby.jar.

10. At the bottom left of the **New Connection** page, make sure that **User ID** is Administrator. Leave **Password** empty.

11. To verify that the connection is successful, click **Test connection**. If an error message is displayed, retrace your steps.

12. Click **Finish**.

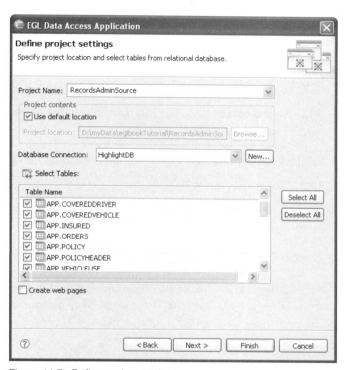

Figure 11.7: Define project settings

13. The **Define project settings** page displays the tables in the database. Select all the tables that are prefixed with APP and click **Next** (Figure 11.7).

14. The **Define the Fields** page displays all the fields in each table. Click **Next**.

15. At the **Define project creation options** page, specify the following package name for the generated code: **highpkg**. Then, select **EGL Services** and check **Qualify table names with schema**. To display a summary page, click **Next**. Then click **Finish**.

Five new packages are in the project RecordsAdminSource, folder EGLSource:

- **highpkg** contains a library that handles exceptions and helps to communicate the status of database-access operations. Also present are Record parts that support these behaviors.

- **highpkg.access** contains the source for the data-access services.

- **highpkg.data** contains the Record parts that are used to create SQL records.

- **highpkg.handlers** contains Interface parts that represent the data-access services.

- **highpkg.primitivetypes.data** contains the data items used in the Record part definitions.

You might review the packages to see how the code is structured.

Create the Source for the Business Service

We now create the service **RecordsAdminService**, which oversees the data-access services to provide data that's meaningful to a requester. For illustration purposes, the service returns a list of insured.

Do as follows:

1. In the project **RecordsAdminSource**, expand **EGLSource**

2. Right-click **highpkg.access**

3. Click **New > Service**. The New EGL Service Part wizard is displayed with the package name already specified as highpkg.access.

4. Name the source file **RecordsAdminService** and check the box **Create as web service**. In this way, you ensure that a WSDL definition is created for you and that the EGL deployment descriptor will indicate that the service is a Web service.

5. Click **Finish**. The file **RecordsAdminService.egl** is displayed, including the Service part of the same name.

6. Update the code as follows.

```
package highpkg.access;

import highpkg.primitivetypes.data.*;
import highpkg.data.*;
import highpkg.*;

Service RecordsAdminService

  use ConditionHandlingLib;

  insuredService InsuredService {@bindService};

  function GetAllInsuredCustomers
          (insuredArray Insured[] out, status StatusRec)
      insuredService.GetInsuredListAll(insuredArray, status);
  end
end
```

Listing 11.1: RecordsAdminService.egl

If a red mark appears at the left, hover over it to read an error message; and then make a change, as appropriate. A correction removes the red mark.

7. Save and close the file.

You may notice an error in the EGL Generation Results view: *Generation failed for RecordsAdminSource.* You earlier informed RBD that you intend to generate a Web service, but you haven't identified the Web project that will receive the generated code. You'll create the project next.

Create the Target Project for the Services

To create the project that will contain the generated Java code for the services you just created, do as follows:

1. From the top menu, click **File > New > Project** and, at the **New Project** dialog, expand **EGL**

2. Select **EGL Project** and click **Next**

3. Type the Project name **RecordsAdmin**

4. Click **Web Project**

5. Click **Next**, and under **Target Runtime**, verify the reference to **WebSphere Application Server v6.1**

6. Click **Finish**

7. Click **Yes** to open the Web perspective, which is used for developing EGL Web-based code

Provide Runtime Access to the Database

The next task is to ensure that the service can access the database at run time. The EGL Runtime Data Source dialog automates the steps that would otherwise be required to update the EGL build descriptor and the two JEE deployment descriptors.

Do as follows:

1. In the Project Explorer, right-click **RecordsAdmin**

2. Click **Properties**

3. At the Properties for RecordsAdmin dialog, click **EGL Runtime Data Source**

4. At the Connection drop-down list, select **HighlightDB**

5. Click **OK**

6. Click **Yes** to update the project's build descriptor

Configure and Generate the Source Project

We'll show you how to prepare to generate output from one project to another and then how to generate.

Configure the EGL Deployment Descriptor

We will deploy RecordsAdminService as a Web service and will deploy InsuredService as an EGL service that is local to the Web service. These details will be known at deployment time if the EGL deployment descriptor is configured as follows:

1. Expand the project **RecordsAdminSource**, then **EGLSource**.

2. Double-click **RecordsAdminSource.egldd**. The file name reflects the project name, and the file type for any EGL deployment descriptor is **.egldd**. The EGL Deployment Descriptor Overview is displayed.

3. To define how EGL-generated logic invokes a service, click the **Service Client Bindings** tab at the bottom of the editor and then click **Add**. The intent here is to create the relationship between RecordsAdminService and InsuredService.

4. At the **Add a Service Client Binding** dialog, click **EGL Binding**, then **Next**. **RecordsAdminService** and **InsuredService** will exchange data that's in a proprietary EGL format.

5. At the **Add an EGL Binding** dialog, click **Browse** and select **InsuredService** from the list; not **IInsuredService**, which refers to the related Interface part. Click **OK**, then **Finish**.

6. Click the **Web Service Deployment** tab. Note that RBD automatically added **RecordsAdminService** and will generate it as a Web service.

7. Save and close the file.

Configure the EGL Build Descriptor

Do as follows:

1. Ensure that the following are expanded in the Project Explorer: **RecordsAdminSource** and the subordinate **EGLSource**. Double-click **RecordsAdminSource.eglbld**, which is the build file. The Build Descriptor editor is displayed.

2. Select the option **genProject**, which identifies the project that receives the generated Java code. Double-click **RecordsAdminSource** to make additional projects available. Click the arrow and select **RecordsAdmin** as the target project.

3. Scroll down to the option **j2ee**, which identifies whether the output is for a JEE environment. Double-click **NO**, click the arrow, and select **YES**.

4. At the top of the options list, click the down arrow for Load DB options using Connections; then select **HighlightDB**. Several build descriptor options are updated.

    We need to specify other build descriptor options, as required for generating a Web service. This step is unnecessary in the usual scenario, when you are generating Web-based output to a Web project also used for developing source code.

5. Clear the check box for **Show only specified options**. Additional build descriptor options are made available to you.

6. Scroll down to the option **serverType**, which identifies the target platform. Double-click **(no value set)**, click the arrow, and select **WEBSPHERE 6.x**.

7. Scroll down to the option **sqlJNDIName**, which specifies a logical name for the database used by the generated service at run time. An important issue here is that a Java Naming and Directory Interface (JNDI) name is case sensitive.

    Click **(no value set)** and type **jdbc/HighlightDB** with the exact case that was specified in the connection name used earlier; specifically, the connection name that you specified when working with EGL Runtime Data Source.

8. Check the box for **Show only specified options**. The only build descriptor options displayed are those for which a value is set. The build descriptor options are now as shown in Figure 11.8.

Figure 11.8: Build Descriptor for RecordsAdminSource

9.   Save and close the file.

Generate the Services

To generate the data-access and business services from project
RecordsAdminSource into the target project:

1.   Go to the Project Explorer

2.   Right-click **RecordsAdminSource**

3.   Click **Generate**

4.   Review the EGL Generation Results view toward the bottom right of
     the EGL perspective. The error message noted earlier is now gone.
     The business service—a Web service—is being generated into a Web

project, along with a local data-access service deployed as an EGL service.

Access the Business Service from the Web

You can now make a service accessible from the Web application. Close all files other than **allInsured.jsp**.

Provide Access to RecordsAdminSource

The EGL JSF handler **allInsured** retrieves data from the service **RecordsAdminService**. The Service part is not defined in HighlightUI, nor is the type of the retrieved data. However, those definitions are already available in project **RecordsAdminSource**.

To provide access to the data types in RecordsAdminSource, update the HighlightUI build path as follows:

1. In the Project Explorer, right-click **HighlightUI** and click **Properties**. The **Properties for HighlightUI** page is displayed.

2. Click **EGL Build Path,** The **EGL Build Path** pane is displayed.

3. On the **Projects** tab, select the check box for **RecordsAdminSource** and click **OK**.

Configure the EGL Deployment Descriptor

To provide runtime access from the Web application to **ResourceAdminService**, configure the EGL deployment descriptor for HighlightUI:

1. In the Project Explorer, navigate to project **HighlightUI**, folder **EGLSource**. Double-click **HighlightUI.egldd**. The Deployment Descriptor editor opens. We'll add the runtime connection to **RecordsAdminService**.

2. In the DeploymentDescriptor editor, click the **Service Client Bindings** tab, then click **Add**.

3. At the **Add a Service Client Binding** dialog, click **Web Binding**, then **Next**. The **Configure Web Service Binding and Interface** dialog is displayed.

4. Check the box labeled **Choose wsdl file from workspace and copy it to the current project**.

5. Click **Browse** to display the Browse WSDL File dialog. Expand the entry for the project **RecordsAdmin**, then expand **WebContent**, **WEB-INF**, and **wsdl**. Click **RecordsAdminService.wsdl**, then **OK**. The **Configure Web Service Binding and Interface** dialog is active again.

6. Do not click **Generate EGL Interface from WSDL file**. Instead, click **Use existing EGL Interface** to specify either an Interface or Service part, which will be available to you in the Deployment Descriptor editor. No EGL part will be copied into HighlightUI.

   Next to the **EGL Interface** field, click **Browse**. At the EGL Interface Selection page, select the Service part **RecordsAdminService** and click **OK**. To finish adding the binding, click **Finish**.

7. Save and close the file.

Revise the Web Page

We'll include controls on the Web page and bind them to variables in the EGL JSF handler.

If **allInsured.jsp** is not open, access it from the Project Explorer by first expanding **HighlightUI** and **WebContent** in turn, and then by clicking **allInsured.jsp**.

Revise the JSF Handler

To revise the JSF handler:

1. Right-click the Web-page surface and click **Edit Page Code**. The JSF handler named **allInsured** is now available in the EGL editor.

   ```
   package jsfhandlers;

   handler allInsured type JSFHandler
       { onstructionFunction = onConstruction,
         onPrerenderFunction = onPrerender,
         view = "allInsured.jsp" }

       // Function Declarations
       function onConstruction()
       end
       function onPrerender()
       end
   end
   ```

2. In the line that precedes the comment for the function declarations, add 2 blank lines and, at the first, type the characters **rec** and press **Ctrl+space**. You've added a variable to access the service RecordsAdminService.

   ```
   recordsAdminService RecordsAdminService {@bindService};
   ```

3. Press ENTER, then type **ins** and press **Ctrl+space**. Select the entry for the Record part named **Insured**. Change the declaration so that the name is **insuredArray** and the type is an array of Insured records.

   ```
   insuredArray Insured[]{};
   ```

4. Move to the end of the line and press **ENTER** to go to the next line in the service.

5. Type the characters **st** and press **Ctrl+space**. Of the displayed choices, double-click the following one.

   ```
   StatusRec - highpkg (record)
   ```

Content assist adds the variable.

6. Include the following code in the **onPrerender** function.

```
try

   onException (except ServiceInvocationException)
      SysLib.setError(except.message);
end
```

7. Now we'll create an error.

Before the onException block, type **records** and press **Ctrl+space**. In this case, you'll choose the second choice, which identifies the service variable you declared earlier, for **RecordsAdminService**. Type a period and press **Ctrl+space** again and double-click the function offered. Your code now references the only function in that service. Place a semicolon at the end of the function invocation and save the file.

```
function onPrerender()
   try
      recordsAdminService.GetAllInsuredCustomers
         (insuredArray, status);
       onException (except ServiceInvocationException)
          SysLib.setError(except.message);
      end
   end
```

A red circle and an underlined word indicate that an error has occurred. Hover over the circle to see the issue: **status** is unresolved. Return to the declaration of **statusRec**, change the variable name to **status** there, and save the file. The error is gone.

When writing code, you may want to find a part definition or variable declaration. The F3 key makes this easy:

1. Double-click **StatusRec** to select that Record part name and press F3. The file **ConditionHandlingLib.egl** is displayed.

2. Highlight that file in the Project Explorer by going to the Project Explorer tool bar and clicking the Link Editor icon (double arrows), if the linking is not already enabled.

Add Controls to the Web Page

We'll add controls to the Web page in a way that binds those controls to variables in the JSF handler:

1. In the editor area, click the tab for **allInsured.jsp**. At the bottom left of your screen is the Page Data view, which provides access to variable declarations. If you cannot find that view, click **Window > Show View > Page Data**.

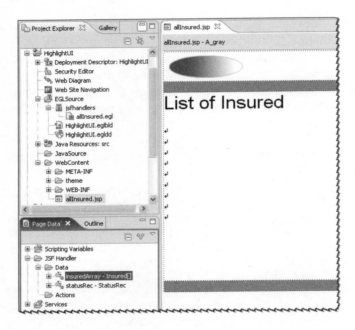

Figure 11.9: Page Data view

2. In the Page Data view, expand **JSF Handler** and **Data**. Select **insuredArray**, which refers to a variable you just created in the JSF handler. Expand **insuredArray** to see the fields in that record (Figure 11.9).

3. Drag **insuredArray** to the Design surface that's shown for **allInsured.jsp**; specifically, to the line after "List of insured." The **Configure Data Controls** page is displayed.

4. For EGL work, use one of two radio-button choices: **Displaying an existing record**, to ensure that all Web-page fields you create during a drag-and-drop operation are read only; or **Updating an existing record**, to allow user input. For now, select the former, which adds read-only controls and does not add any buttons to the Web page.

5. You can choose which record fields to use. We want only a few, so clear all the choices by clicking **None**, then click Lastname, Firstname, and Email.

6. You can customize the controls you're creating. Highlight the row for **Firstname**, click the **Label** column, and change the label to **First name**. Do the same for **Lastname**.

7. You can change the order of the columns that will be displayed on the Web page. Highlight the row for **Firstname** and click the up-arrow to the right of the row so that the order of fields is **Firstname**, then **Lastname**.

8. To place the controls on the Web page, click **Finish**.

9. Save the page.

Prepare to Run the Web Application

You can ensure that your code is up to date by rebuilding the workspace. Here's the procedure:

1. From the top menu, click **Project > Clean**

2. At the Clean dialog, select **Clean all projects** and click **OK**

Next, place the services on the server:

1. If the server is not started, click **Start**. The icon is a white triangle embedded in a green circle.

2. At the Servers view, right-click the server and click **Add and Remove projects**. The **Add and Remove** dialog is displayed.

3. Highlight **RecordsAdminEar** and click **Add**.

4. Click **Finish**.

Run the Web Application

To run the Web application:

1. In the editor area, click the tab for **allInsured.jsp**.

2. If the JSP file is not highlighted in Project Explorer, click the Link Edit icon (two arrows).

3. In the Project Explorer, right-click the highlighted file and click **Run As > Run on Server**.

4. Your Web page should be displayed, with data from **RecordsAdminService**.

   If your Web page did not display successfully, reset your environment and try again:

   a. Go to the Servers view at the bottom of Rational Business Developer and right-click **WebSphere Application Server v6.1**

   b. Select **Add and Remove Projects**

   c. At the **Add and Remove Projects** page, click **Remove All**, then **Finish**

   d. Select **Add and Remove Projects** again

   e. At the **Add and Remove Projects** page, add **RecordsAdminEAR** and click **Finish**

   f. In the Project Explorer, right-click **allInsured.jsp** and click **Run As > Run on Server**

Create an Integration Service

The fourth project holds the files for a Web service that sends greetings to every Highlight Insurance policy holder.

Create the Project CustomerContact

To create the project CustomerContact:

1. In the Project Explorer, right-click a blank area.

2. Click **New > Project** and, at the New Project dialog, expand **EGL**.

3. Click **EGL Project**, then **Next;** alternatively, double-click **EGL Project**. The **New EGL Project** page is displayed.

4. Type the Project name as follows: **CustomerContact.**

5. Click **Web Project**.

6. Click **Next**, and under **Target Runtime**, accept **WebSphere Application Server v6.1**.

7. Click **Finish**.

Create the Service CustomerContactService

A service designer might provide an interface to a service developer, who would then *implement* the interface; that is, create a service that includes the operations specified in the interface. We'll fulfill both roles, designing an Interface part and then using the Interface part to begin writing the service.

Create the Interface CustomerContactInterface

To create the Interface part, do as follows:

1. Expand **CustomerContact**.

2. Right-click **EGLSource**.

3. Click **New > Interface**.

4. At the **New EGL Interface Part** dialog, type the source-file name **CustomerContactInterface**, set the package name to **interfaces**, and click **Finish**. The Interface part named **CustomerContactInterface** is now available in the EGL editor.

   RBD has created an EGL file with the same name as the Interface part and placed it in the following location: under folder EGLSource and, within that folder, in the **interfaces** package.

5. Specify a signature for the operation that you want the service to implement. The changed code is shown here, in boldface.

```
package interfaces;

// interface
interface CustomerContactInterface

    function SendGreetingToAll(msgType int in) returns(int);

end
```

6. Save and close the file.

Create a Service to Implement the Interface

To create the Web service to implement CustomerContactInterface, do as follows:

1. Expand **CustomerContact**.

2. Right-click **EGLSource**.

3. Click **New > Service**.

4. At the **New EGL Service Part** dialog, type the source-file name **CustomerContactService** and set the package name to **services**.

5. Click the **Add** button to display the **Implemented Interfaces Selection** dialog. Click **CustomerContactInterface** and click **OK**.

6. Click the check box for **Create as web service** and click **Finish**. The Service part named **CustomerContactService** is now available in the EGL editor, including a comment to indicate a task to do.

```
package services;

import interfaces.CustomerContactInterface;

service CustomerContactService
   implements CustomerContactInterface

   function SendGreetingToAll(msgType int in) returns (int)
     // TODO Auto-generated function
   end

end
```

RBD has created an EGL file with the same name as the Service part and placed the file in the following location: under folder EGLSource and, within that folder, in the **services** package.

In the service **CustomerContactService**, we'll update the function **SendGreetingsToAll** and show a benefit of using content assist.

Provide Access to RecordsAdminSource

The service **CustomerContactService** retrieves data from the service **RecordsAdminService**. Required data definitions are already available in project **RecordsAdminSource**. To provide access to the part definitions in **RecordsAdminSource**, we now update the CustomerContact build path.

Here's the procedure:

1. In the Project Explorer, right-click **CustomerContact** and click **Properties**. The **Properties for CustomerContact** dialog is displayed.

2. Click **EGL Build Path**, The EGL Build Path dialog is displayed.

3. Check the box for **RecordsAdminSource** and click **OK**.

Write the Service Code

Our current project has access to the EGL data types in RecordsAdminSource; but our service code still does not. One way to provide the access is to type **import** statements in the service code. Another way is to let content assist add the **import** statements automatically.

Add a Variable Based on a Service

Add two blank lines preceding the function in **CustomerContactService**. On the first, type the characters **rec**, and press **Ctrl+space**. The code changes are shown here in boldface.

```
package services;

import highpkg.access.RecordsAdminService;
import interfaces.CustomerContactInterface;

service CustomerContactService
   implements CustomerContactInterface

   recordsAdminService RecordsAdminService
     {@bindService};

   function SendGreetingToAll(msgType INT IN)
      returns (INT)
    // TODO Auto-generated function
   end

end
```

Save the file.

Add Records

We need to add two variables that are based on Record parts. In each case, we'll use a variable name that's the same as the Record part name:

1. In the line that precedes the function in **CustomerContactService**, type **insured** and press **Ctrl+space**. Of the displayed choices, double-click the following one.

```
Insured - highpkg.data (record)
```

2. Content assist adds the variable declaration and import statement. However, you need to indicate that you are declaring an array. Change the declaration so that the type is an array of Insured records.

```
insured Insured[]{};
```

3. Move to the end of the line, then press **ENTER** to go to the next line in the service.

4. Type the characters **st** and press **Ctrl+space**. Of the displayed choices, double-click the following one.

```
StatusRec - highpkg (record)
```

Content assist adds the variable.

5. Save the file.

The consequence of these steps is that your code includes the following statements.

```
package services;

import highpkg.StatusRec;
import highpkg.access.RecordsAdminService;
import highpkg.data.Insured;
import interfaces.CustomerContactInterface;

service CustomerContactService
    implements CustomerContactInterface
    recordsAdminService RecordsAdminService {@bindService};
    insured Insured[]{};
    statusRec StatusRec;

    function SendGreetingToAll(msgType int in) returns (int)
    //  TODO Auto-generated function
    end
end
```

Complete the function SendGreetingToAll

To complete the function **SendGreetingToAll**, type the code shown.

```
Function SendGreetingToAll(msgType int in) returns (int)
   Greeting string;
   case(msgType)
      when(1)
         Greeting = "Happy Holidays!";
      when(2)
         Greeting = "Have a Terrific New Year!";
      otherwise
         Greeting = "Drive Carefully!";
   end

   recordsAdminService.GetAllInsuredCustomers
      (insured, statusRec);

   if(statusRec.succeeded)
      for(count INT from 1 to insured.getSize())
         // send a Greeting to insured[count].FirstName
         ;
      end
      return(1);
   else
      return(0);
   end
end
```

Save the file.

As invoked by a Web application, the function **SendGreetingToAll** receives a number that indicates which of several messages to send to each person insured by Highlight Insurance. An EGL **case** statement selects among the alternatives. The function then invokes the operation **recordsAdminService.GetAllInsuredCustomers**, which returns an array of data necessary to contact those people. If the operation succeeds, SendGreetingToAll sends the requested message to each person in the list and returns control to the Web application.

An important point for our purpose is that **CustomerContactService** is invoking another service; and in this case, the invoked code is deployed as a Web service.

Configure the Deployment Descriptor

To configure the EGL deployment descriptor for CustomerContact, do as follows:

1. Under the CustomerContact project and EGLSource folder, double-click **CustomerContact.egldd**. The file name reflects the project name, and the file type for any EGL deployment descriptor is **.egldd**. The **EGL Deployment Descriptor Overview** is displayed.

2. To define how **CustomerContactService** itself invokes a service, click the **Service Client Bindings** tab and then click **Add**. The intent here is to create the relationship between **CustomerContactService** and **RecordsAdminService**.

3. At the **Add a Service Client Binding** dialog, click **Web Binding**, then **Next**. The **Configure Web Service Binding and Interface** dialog is displayed.

4. Check the box labeled **Choose wsdl file from workspace and copy it to the current project**. The WSDL file you access will be brought into your project and will be present at deployment time. At run time, the WSDL file provides the detail necessary for **CustomerContactService** to access **RecordsAdminService**.

5. Click **Browse** to display the **Browse WSDL File** dialog. Your goal now is to access the WSDL definition that the EGL generator created for **RecordsAdminService**. Expand the entry for the project **RecordsAdmin**, then expand **WebContent**, **WEB-INF**, and **wsdl**. Click **RecordsAdminService.wsdl**, then **OK**. The **Configure Web Service Binding and Interface** dialog is active again.

6. Do not generate an interface from the WSDL. Instead, click **Use existing EGL Interface** to specify either an Interface or Service part.

   Click **Browse**, and, at the EGL Interface Selection page, select the Service part **RecordsAdminService** and click **OK**. To finish adding the binding, click **Finish**.

7. Click the **Web Service Deployment** tab. Note that RBD added **CustomerContactService** and will generate it as a Web service.

8. Save and close the file **CustomerContact.egldd**.

Access Details on Build Descriptor Options

In the Project Explorer, if you double-click the build file **CustomerContact.eglbld**, you'll see the current build descriptor options. No changes are needed. The reference to DB2 has no effect on the generation of **CustomerContactService**, which does not itself access a database.

You can get detailed information on the purpose of a given build descriptor. Click **serverType**, press F1, and at the Related Topics page, click **serverType** to read about that option. For an overview of the build descriptor, click the browser back-arrow to return to the Related Topics page; then, click **Build descriptor options**.

Generate the Project CustomerContact

To generate the integration service in project CustomerContact, go to the Project Explorer, right-click **CustomerContact**, and click **Generate**.

Complete the Web Application

We'll now do the steps necessary to complete HighlightUI, including using a WSDL definition to create an Interface part for use by the Web application. In this way, we show how you can use EGL to interact with a Web service that's written in any language.

Complete the EGL Deployment Descriptor

To configure the EGL deployment descriptor for HighlightUI, do as follows:

1. In the Project Explorer, navigate to project **HighlightUI**, folder **EGLSource**. Double-click **HighlightUI.egldd**. The Deployment Descriptor editor opens. We've already handled the connection for **RecordsAdminService** and will now add one for **CustomerContactService**.

2. In the DeploymentDescriptor editor, click the **Service Client Bindings** tab, then click **Add**.

3. At the Add a Service Client Binding dialog, click **Web Binding**, then **Next**. The Configure Web Service Binding and Interface dialog is displayed.

4. Check the box labeled **Choose wsdl file from workspace and copy it to the current project**.

5. Click **Browse** to display the Browse WSDL File dialog. Expand the entry for the project **CustomerContact**, then expand **WebContent**, **WEB-INF**, and **wsdl**. Click **CustomerContactService.wsdl**, then **OK**. The **Add a Service Client Binding** dialog is active again.

6. Ensure that the radio button is selected for **Generate EGL Interface from WSDL File**. Click **Next** twice. The **New EGL Interface** page is displayed.

    Your purpose in creating an Interface part from the WSDL definition is to use that part as the basis of a variable in your EGL JSF handler. In this case, we're following the usual procedure for interacting with Web services.

    We'll put the new Interface part in a package named **interfaces**, but will retain the default name of the Interface part: **CustomerContactService**.

7. In the New EGL Interface page, rename the package from services to **interfaces**.

8. Click **Finish** and then save and close the EGL deployment descriptor.

Complete the EGL JSF Handler

To complete the EGL JSF handler:

1. Right click the **allInsured.jsp** Web-page surface and click **Edit Page Code**. The handler named **allInsured** is now available in the EGL editor. Expand the import statement to show all import statements.

```
package jsfhandlers;

import highpkg.StatusRec;
import highpkg.access.RecordsAdminService;
import highpkg.data.Insured;

handler allInsured type JSFHandler
    {onConstructionFunction = onConstruction,
        onPrerenderFunction = onPrerender,
        view = "allInsured.jsp"}

    recordsAdminService RecordsAdminService{@bindService};
    insuredArray Insured[]{};
    status StatusRec;

    function onConstruction()
    end

    function onPrerender()
        try
            recordsAdminService.GetAllInsuredCustomers
                (insuredArray, status);
            onException(except ServiceInvocationException)
                SysLib.setError(except.message);
        end
    end
end
```

2. In the line that precedes the declaration for **recordsAdminService**, add a blank line and type the characters **cus** and press **Ctrl+space**. You've added a variable to access the service **CustomerContactService**.

```
customerContactService CustomerContactService
    {@bindService};
```

3. Add three more global variables, as shown here.

```
msgStatus INT;
msgInput INT {DisplayUse = input,
                DisplayName = "Message Input"};
msgText STRING{DisplayUse = output,
                DisplayName = "Message Sent?"};
```

4. Add the function **respondToButtonClick**, as shown here.

```
function respondToButtonClick()
   try
      msgStatus =
         customerContactService.SendGreetingToAll(msgInput);
      onException (except ServiceInvocationException)
         sysLib.setError(except.message);
         msgStatus = 16;
   end
   case (msgStatus)
      when(1)
         msgText = "Yes!";
      when(0)
         mgText = "No!";
      otherwise
         msgText = "Service invocation failed!";
   end
end
```

5. Save the file.

Complete the Web Page

To complete the Web page:

1. Click the tab for **allInsured.jsp**. At the bottom left of your screen is the Page Data view, which provides access to variable declarations. If you cannot find that view, click **Window > Show View > Page Data**.

2. In the Page Data view, expand **Data**, select **msgInput**, and drag it a line or two below the Web-page fields you placed in **allInsured.jsp**. The Configure Data Controls page is displayed.

3. Select **Updating an existing record**.

4. Click **Options**. The Options dialog is displayed.

5. In the Buttons tab, clear the check boxes so that no buttons are created. In the Labels tab, ensure that you are not appending a colon to a label. Click **OK**, then **Finish**. Now that you have an initial input field, the Page Designer places an error-message field on the page.

6. On the Web page, press Tab four times so that the cursor is at the left of the error-message field. Press ENTER four times to leave room between the input field and the error-message field.

7. Right-click the error-message field and click **Properties**. At the left of the Properties view is a tab for the JSF tag h:message. Ensure that the radio button on the right is set for **Show all error messages generated by this page**.

8. In the Page Data view, select **msgText** and, in the same way, place it a line or two after the Web field related to msgInput. The annotation **DisplayUse** (as you typed in the JSF handler) ensures that the field is for output. Click **Finish**.

9. Click in the middle of the right border of the output box that's bound to **msgText**. Extend the box slightly to the right.

10. In the Page Data view, expand **Actions** and drag **respondToButton** in between the output box and the error-message box. Right-click that button and click **Properties**. In the Properties view, click **Display options** and replace the content of the **Button label** field with Submit.

11. Save the page.

Prepare to Run the Web Application

To place the services on the server:

1. If the server is not started, start it.

2. In the Servers view at the bottom of Rational Business Developer, right-click **WebSphere Application Server v6.1**, click **Add and Remove Projects**. The **Add and Remove Projects** dialog is displayed.

3. Highlight **CustomerContactEar** and click **Add**. All three EAR files should now be on the right.

4. Click **Finish**.

Run the Web Application

To run the Web application:

1. In the edit area, click the tab for **allInsured.jsp**.

2. In the Project Explorer toolbar, if the behavior of the Link Edit icon (two arrows) is not enabled, click the icon.

3. In the Project Explorer, right-click the highlighted file and click **Run As > Run on Server**.

4. Your Web page should be displayed, with data from **RecordsAdminService**.

5. Type **7** in the text box for Message Input. Click **Submit**. The content in **Message Sent?** should be **Yes!** Close the browser.

6. Repeat the run. In the Project Explorer, right-click the highlighted file and click **Run As > Run on Server**.

7. The number **7** remains in the text box because the handler is in session scope and was never destroyed, but provided data to the component tree in the first phase of the JSF lifecycle. Close the browser.

8. To destroy the handler, do as follows in the Servers view: expand the server, right-click **HighlightUIEAR**, and click **Restart HighlightUIEAR**. Wait for the server to finish processing.

9. Repeat the run. In the Project Explorer, right-click the highlighted file and click **Run As > Run on Server**.

10. The page is displayed as it was during the first run. Close the browser.

11. In the Servers view, expand the server, right-click **CustomerContactEAR**, click **Remove**, and at the confirmation message, click **OK**. Wait for the server to finish processing.

12. Type **7** in the text box for **Message Input** and click **Submit**. The content after **Message Sent?** should be **Service Invocation Failed!** EGL error messages should be displayed after the button.

13. To correct the problem:

    a. In the Servers view, right-click the server and click **Add and Remove Projects**. The **Add and Remove Projects** dialog is displayed.

    b. Highlight **CustomerContactEar** and click **Add**.

    c. Click **Finish**.

APPENDIX A

Sources of Information

S everal sources of information are available on Rational Business Developer, EGL, and the technologies featured in this book.

Rational Business Developer

The primary Web site for Rational Business Developer is here:

http://www.ibm.com/developerworks/rational/products/rbde

When you visit, look for a link to the EGL Cafe, which is a spiffy interactive site dedicated to news on the language.

EGL Rich UI

Details on EGL Rich UI are at the following site:

http://www.alphaworks.ibm.com/tech/reglrws

MC Press

The MC Press site includes the database needed to work through the Chapter 10 tutorial and may include additional details on this book:

http://www.mc-store.com/5087.html

Eclipse and BIRT

Rational Business Developer is built on Eclipse. You don't need to download Eclipse separately, but might want to learn more about the platform:

http://www.eclipse.org

Also on that site is information on Business Intelligence and Reporting Tools (BIRT), including a tutorial:

http://www.eclipse.org/birt/phoenix/

Apache Derby

For details and upgrade information on the database management system Apache Derby, see the following Web site:

http://db.apache.org/derby

JavaServer Faces

JavaServer Faces Specification Version 1.1 by Sun Microsystems, Inc., is at the following Web site: i

http://java.sun.com/javaee/javaserverfaces/download.html

Index